HIGH-VALUE VEGGIES

BY MEL BARTHOLOMEW

635 BAR
Bartholomew, Mel.
Square foot gardening
  high-value veggies

CENTRAL $17.99
          31994015491704

COOL
SPRINGS
PRESS
Home and Garden Experts™
MINNEAPOLIS, MINNESOTA

Quarto is the authority on a wide range of topics.

Quarto educates, entertains and enriches the lives of
our readers—enthusiasts and lovers of hands-on living.

www.quartoknows.com

First published in 2016 by Cool Springs Press, an imprint of Quarto Publishing Group USA Inc.,
400 First Avenue North, Suite 400, Minneapolis, MN 55401 USA. Telephone: (612) 344-8100 Fax: (612) 344-8692

quartoknows.com
Visit our blogs at quartoknows.com

10 9 8 7 6 5 4 3 2

ISBN: 978-1-59186-668-8

Library of Congress Cataloging-in-Publication Data

Names: Bartholomew, Mel, author.
Title: Square foot gardening high-value veggies : homegrown produce ranked by value / Mel Bartholomew.
Description: Minneapolis, MN : Cool Springs Press, 2016.
Identifiers: LCCN 2015040351 | ISBN 9781591866688 (pb)
Subjects: LCSH: Vegetable gardening--Economic aspects. | Square foot
  gardening. | Rate of return.
Classification: LCC SB320.9 .B37 2016 | DDC 635--dc23
LC record available at http://lccn.loc.gov/2015040351

Acquiring Editor: Mark Johanson
Project Manager: Alyssa Bluhm
Art Director: Cindy Samargia Laun
Book Design and Layout: Simon Larkin
Cover Photography: Paul Markert

SPECIAL THANKS TO THE FOLLOWING
CONTRIBUTORS: W. Atlee Burpee & Company,
Shawna Coronado, Rosalind Creasy, Chelsey Fields,
Carolyn Henry-Johanson, Janine Larson, Sharon
Lovejoy, Elizabeth Murphy, Jason Stoneburner

Printed in China

CONTENTS

INTRODUCTION   PAGE 4

SECTION **1**   WHAT IS A SMART   PAGE 8
                GARDEN INVESTMENT?

SECTION **2**   HIGH-VALUE VEGGIES: PAGE 26
                THE WINNERS!

SECTION **3**   OTHER KINDS OF VALUE   PAGE 94

Mel Bartholomew doing what he likes best: relaxing in a lush Square Foot Garden.

INTRODUCTION

I've been gardening for more than 70 years. Over all those years, I've worked with or taught more novice gardeners than I can count. I've been around the world spreading the gardening gospel, and I can tell you, it always starts with one simple question: "What should I grow?" I bet you think that's an easy one. Well, think again.

The answer I usually give is: "It depends." Where do you live? What are your favorite vegetables? What would your family prefer to eat? How much money could you save on groceries? How much room do you have in your yard to dedicate to a garden and what sun exposure does it receive? Any of these, and more to boot, could affect your decision.

But I've come to believe that one of the best ways to determine what to grow, a way that works for every gardener and every garden, is to ask yourself, "What are the most valuable crops I could harvest?" One of the reasons many people garden, after all, is to save some money on their grocery bills. If you decide to grow zucchini rather than carrots, you're going to have to buy your carrots. But would it be smarter to grow carrots and buy your zucchini? That's a dollars-and-sense calculation well worth making. Unfortunately, it's the type of calculation that most gardeners I've met just never make. They wouldn't know where to start.

You start with the numbers. I like numbers, and I like making them work for me. That's how I became a successful engineer, and that's how I was able to invent a brand new way to garden. After all, you can tell just from its name that Square Foot Gardening is all about numbers.

But here's why I wrote this book. One of the very best answers to, "What should I grow?" is, "The crops that will bring you the biggest return on your investment." It's not easy figuring out what your payback for every potential fruit or vegetable might be. You need to figure out how much yield you're going to get in a given season versus how much time, effort, and how many resources you're going to put into growing that vegetable. You'll need to find out the going market rate per pound for the vegetable, and then relate that price to the amount you can reasonably grow in a season. You can get a headache doing all that math. No need to reach for the aspirin, though; I've done the math for you.

Just looking through a seed catalog or taking a trip to the local nursery can overwhelm someone confronted with the amazing number of options gardeners have to choose from. Next, visit a farmer's market and a grocery store in the same town and you'll understand the wide diversity of prices for the same edible. Figuring all that into your garden's return on investment involves a lot of calculations. But now, you'll find all the calculations boiled down in one easy resource—this book.

Fresh produce is expensive, plain and simple. Most of us are willing to pay the price because there is nothing better in the whole-food world. But instead of paying four bucks for a few leaves of kale, more people are choosing to grow their own veggies. In fact, every year there are around 800,000 first-time gardeners in the USA. But just as you need to pay attention to prices and be a smart shopper at the market, you need to make smart investment decisions when you're planning and planting your garden.

Build a box. Fill the box with Mel's Mix. Add a grid and start planting. That's Square Foot Gardening (SFG) in a nutshell. But even if you don't use the SFG method (and why wouldn't you want to?), you still need to think about *return on investment* (ROI). The information in this book is just as useful for gardeners who grow in containers or straw bales or even rows as it is for SFG growers. It's all about the ROI, after all.

MY STORY

My interest in gardening started at a young age, watching my mother tend our backyard garden in Buffalo, New York. When we moved to San Gabriel, California, we could be outdoors all year round, and I was assigned garden duties. World War II brought Victory Gardens. Our next move took us to Ridgewood, New Jersey, where I did so much weeding and heavy work that I came to hate gardening. It was time I could have spent playing ball. When I left for college I vowed, "I will never garden again!" As the years went by, I moved my own family several times, started my own business, and was too busy for much more than a tomato patch. I sold my company and retired at 42 and decided to rediscover gardening as a hobby. As a trained engineer, I was always looking for efficiency in the numbers. That's what led me to found Square Foot Gardening, the method that led me to write several bestselling books, film several TV shows, and start a nonprofit foundation. I wanted to design a better way to garden to get a bigger yield with less work. I didn't want to waste any time, effort, money, or space. Why would you want to plant a lot of one crop that takes a long time to mature or has little food value or takes an inordinate amount of water or fertilizer compared to its yield? When I was learning and listening to experts, I kept thinking, "this is all backwards. It's not how much you want to plant, or how long the rows are, it should be how much you want to harvest and even more important, what value are you getting for all your efforts?" That led me to think about the best crop to plant for the best dollar return and yield! I found that in Square Foot Gardening.

HOW TO USE THIS BOOK

I've asked my good friend and fellow writer Chris Peterson to help me research the information and crunch the numbers for the comparison tables. Together, we have laid out the meat of the subject so that you don't necessarily need to read the book all the way through. Sure, you can start with Section 1 and find out what drives the calculations we had to make and what the variables are. If you're like me, you'll find that stuff pretty interesting, and the information lays down a good, solid foundation for understanding what we mean when we say "smart garden investment." But if you're like a lot of gardeners I know, you may be chomping at the bit to figure out the plants that work best for you. If that's the case, you can just jump right into Section 2, where you'll find the actual plant listings themselves. We've put the top ten ranked plants—according to the actual dollar return on your investment—right at the front of the section. The plant listings themselves are organized according to their rank (you'll find an alphabetical index on page 93).

Once you've got to the point where you've narrowed your search for this season's plants, you can consult Section 3, where you'll find other a lot of other ways to look at high value. We've included several "Top 10" lists to help you make all kinds of other decisions.

WHO KNOWS MORE ABOUT FOOD VALUE THAN A CHEF?

Jason Stoneburner, the executive chef of Bastille Café and Bar in Seattle, Washington, chooses plants for the restaurant's expansive rooftop garden with value foremost in his mind. The idea of fresh, organic greens and veggies just a staircase away is appealing, but the garden takes a lot of planning, work, and resources. Jason makes sure it provides tangible return on that investment. Managing the restaurant's rooftop garden is a lesson in screening plant choices through the thoughtful lens of value to meet specific needs. It's a lesson we can all benefit from.

For Stoneburner, value translates to a quick and usable harvest. "It's about getting as much of the rooftop produce onto diners' plates. So we have to grow crops that mature quickly." Stoneburner harvests the vegetables young, serving baby turnips and baby carrots—a strategy

that any home gardener and cook could use to plant and harvest multiple crops in the same season.

Admittedly, the chef has a slightly different idea of value than the home gardener and cook might. "We try to plant things that we can harvest and put on a plate with minimal effort. Like different varieties of lettuces. We can charge somebody for a bowl of lettuces. But it's hard to charge for herbs, because they are a specific ingredient that isn't a main focal point of the dish."

Any home gardener can, however, use Bastille's strategy of growing unusual species and varieties that are easy to prepare and exceptional on their own. One example is substituting for standard bell peppers with Padron peppers, a much more flavorful and adaptable option. Stoneburner finds these incredibly useful in his kitchen. "Padron peppers are a Basque heirloom pepper

grown very small and served simply. They are the perfect pepper because you can eat them whole, enjoy them with a beer or a glass of wine."
—*Chris Peterson*

WHAT IS A SMART GARDEN INVESTMENT?

How do you determine value in what you plant, cultivate, and grow? That's a great question, and it just might be the perfect question for any gardener to start with. For a lot of the gardeners I've met, value starts with the joy of growing something you usually have to buy, and that tastes a whole lot better than most store-bought produce. Getting back to the land, the pleasure of getting your hands deep into the soil, and accomplishing something profound can all be valuable parts of gardening too. But as wonderful as that all is, as valuable as it might be, it's mighty hard to measure. If you're like most people, the "value" of your garden investment can more easily be broken down and measured in the actual price you can put on the produce you grow. Put in more practical terms: how much money are you going to save?

Let's face it, anything you grow and eat is something you don't have to buy. Even though you'll put a good deal of work into a garden—along with tangible

Although the return on investment you get from planting a garden can be calculated many ways, the best way to make an objective comparison between, say, tomatoes and broccoli, is to crunch some numbers.

investments including plants or seeds, soil amendments, and gallon upon gallon of water—you'll usually get a decent return on your investment. However, it's important to understand that this isn't always the case. It all depends on what you grow. I have watched many gardeners simply pick what's easiest or what they think will do best given the local weather, the space they have available in their backyard, and whatever has worked for their neighbors. But here's something I tell all the novice gardeners I meet: keep in mind that the easiest things to grow are also likely to be most widely produced, and are probably vegetables that can be purchased locally at a very low price. The fact is, you might save a lot more money growing something a bit more in demand, something grocery stores and farmer's markets in your area don't regularly carry. Of course, it must be something your family wants to eat or you've wasted your time and money.

No matter what measure you choose to use, the time to figure out the real value of what you grow in your garden is before you ever drop a seed into a hole you've made in your sun-warmed soil. That means relying on numbers. I'm an engineer by training, so I know that numbers don't lie. You just have to get the numbers right, and they'll tell you more than you can imagine. Getting them right in terms of calculating garden value means measuring one thing against the other while making sure that it's a fair comparison. That's what I call "garden investment." At its core, it's a thoughtful approach to edible plant selection with an eye to which plants represent the best use of your time, money, and effort.

That's the theory. In practice, wise garden investment can be broken down into a simple but powerful equation:

The yield per square foot over a full growing season		The average cost per pound at retail		Value of the harvest for one season		The total cost of inputs over the season		The net value of the harvest, or return on investment	ROI
	x		=		−		=		
Thyme 2.00 lbs	x	$42.44	=	$84.88	−	$15.80	=	$69.08	437%

The beauty of the formula is that it works for any plant that produces a crop. It is also scalable; because we've included the projected yield per square foot, you can just multiply the square foot space you're growing in. Like any really useful formula, it's flexible.

The calculations that use this formula, and that form the heart of this book, have been carefully researched to ensure the information for each variable comes from reputable sources and that the sources are comparable in each plant's case.

In simple terms, the calculations take into account what you put into each individual plant subtracted from what the harvest from that plant is worth. It's a fairly simple idea, but the actual calculations are somewhat more complex, dealing with a wide number of variables.

Einstein once said, *"Make things as simple as possible, but no simpler."* That was the challenge we had in actually building a formula that would provide conclusions that readers and gardeners could use to guide their crop decisions, without making the numbers so complex that you would need to be Einstein to figure them out.

MEASURING YOUR GARDEN INVESTMENT

When I started discussing this book with the editors, the first question that came up was: How are we going to actually calculate value? The trick was to create a formula that would work with every edible on a long and diverse list. Of course, no matter what calculations the formula included, we had to make sure that it made an (excuse the pun) apples-to-apples comparison.

I like facts, so it was very important to me to use reliable sources of information that could provide real-world numbers for the listings. We had to use references that worked from a national average, so that the formula would apply to all gardeners across the country. As it turned out, no source—not even the USDA—was comprehensive. In practice, some of the primary sources didn't list information for one edible or another, or didn't provide numbers for one of the key factors in the calculations. For those situations, we had to develop secondary sources that would match the information in the primary sources. There was a lot of looking at databases for just the right starting places.

I like to work with numbers, and I'm comfortable with them. I also know that a lot of people aren't as comfortable. That's why it was essential to me that the formula itself makes sense. I wanted any reader to be able to look at the formula and see how it worked at a glance. It had to be intuitive and it had to be relevant, no matter if you were a first-time gardener, an experienced backyard grower, or even someone with a larger piece of land doing the kind of intensive gardening that could be called small farming.

Basically, we came up with a formula that uses an average price per pound to determine what a season's worth of produce from any given plant is worth. That value is then measured against the cost of inputs to grow the plant over a season, to calculate overall return on investment (ROI) in terms of both an actual dollar figure and a percentage.

That gives you two ways to look at the results: the money in your pocket and the actual return you receive relative to what's put in and market value.

Tempering the Formula

One final word on using the formula as we've presented it here. Although we've taken great care in tying the calculations to real-world numbers, what can't be calculated are personal goals and preferences. Earning money back from what you plant is a great feeling. So is eating well, enjoying the food you eat, showing off your garden to your friends, and sharing what you grow. The point is to never get so focused on profitability and high value that you forget the higher purposes of gardening: to grow nutritious, delicious food with a minimum impact to the environment. In my experience, you can realize a return on your garden investment and meet other important goals at the same time.

GROWING VALUE: A HIGH-VALUE LEDGER

Having grown more gardens than I can count, in more places than you can imagine, I know better than most that the best calculations are the ones that refer to your garden specifically. The strength and weakness of the calculations used in *High Value Veggies* is that they are geared toward a national average. In reality, of course, this is a great big country and prices and growing conditions are different from one place to the next.

That's why I recommend gardeners keep a *garden investment ledger*. A ledger provides a snapshot of how profitable your garden actually is. Record-keeping is crucial if you're going to make adjustments that will help you realize the greatest return on investment from what you grow.

The most important things to log in your ledger are the actual costs. Check local produce prices for the crops you're growing. Note if those prices swing up or down at harvest time. Also keep close track of "inputs" such as a large water bill. Unusual garden expenses can skew the calculations as we've listed them.

It shouldn't take much time to get your ledger in order if you update it as the season moves along. Then, at the end of the season, or during that nice down time in the winter, assess what the ledger tells you and use those results to adjust your plant selections for the next season. I think you'll find that the ledger becomes a gardening tool as important as a trowel!

PRODUCE COST FACTORS

Although some produce is sold by the head, ear, or bunch, most is sold by the pound. All produce can easily be converted to a per-pound equivalent. That's why we decided to use per-pound yields and pricing for the first two columns of our calculations—it was just the obvious choice. Pounds might not equal flavor, and there is no accounting for personal preference, but when it comes to measuring the dollar value of what grows in garden, yield weight is the best common denominator with which to start.

However, it's not as simple as it might seem to calculate the pounds of harvest you can expect from any given plant. Even choices that grow in self-contained units—for instance, carrots—can differ radically in the actual weight of one unit, from variety to variety. Large Scarlet Nantes carrots are several times bigger than ball varieties. A beefsteak tomato is going to be appreciably larger than an Early Girl, not to mention the case of many heirloom tomatoes, which can grow noticeably different-sized fruits on the same plant. Diversity occurs in just about every vegetable.

So, for purposes of the listings and calculations in Section 2, we used the most common varieties that represent the closest possible approximation to what you would find in a grocery produce department.

We then surveyed a range of grocery stores and farmer's markets to determine what the average carrot weighs, or how many Brussels sprouts are in a pound on average. This way, we had a common number for the price per pound, which would relate to the pounds-per-square-foot yield (you didn't think I'd get all the way through this without bringing up "Square Foot" did you?). We then determined the actual

SOME FINE PRINT

One issue that came up in researching the yield weight over a season of different crops involved unit-for-sale versus edible portion. Some agricultural academics go to great lengths to filter down any crop's yield to the "edible portion," the amount leftover when inedible and unusable parts are discarded. This was too problematic to consider for our purposes. Yes, fresh corn produces fewer cups of edible kernels than hulled strawberries do. But both are sold whole at retail. So we used that whole portion as the consistent baseline. For the same reason, we measured and considered only loose produce, not prepackaged. Bags of potatoes or plastic clamshells of trimmed baby lettuce leaves may be widely available at retail, but there are too many variables in those processed products to make for a fair comparison in our calculations.

That said, if you want to drill down in our calculations, and you're adamant about measuring only edible portions of your garden crops, you can create a "weighting factor"—a numerical range of numbers to be subtracted from the yield number based on the portion of any crop that is composted as waste. Seems like a lot of work for very little reward as far as I'm concerned, but I would never stop anybody from working with numbers. This would, however, change the relative position of some crops on the list such as corn and broccoli. But it wouldn't radically affect our Top 10.

yield for a given crop over a standard season by checking academic studies and the yield estimates of seed companies, where available.

Gardeners grow their gardens in lots of different ways. Some grow traditional rows, others grow in containers or raised beds, and those who have read my other books grow hyper-efficient gardens in boxes, square foot by square foot. Fortunately, the production of any of these can be conveniently converted into yield per square foot. As the founder of Square Foot Gardening, I already had access to well-established data on what most edible plants produce in an actual square foot. That gave us a "foot" up in getting the numbers in the formula right.

That Pesky Price Per Pound

Establishing the price for pound we'd use in each case involved even more thought and investigation. Ultimately, we turned to the United States Department of Agriculture's (USDA) Agricultural Marketing Service. The service provides a bi-monthly "National Retail Report" for common fruits and vegetables sold at large retail outlets—namely supermarkets and large clubs such as Costco. The report provides, among other things, a national cost-per-pound average for a wide range of fruits and vegetables. The average is determined from a survey of prices in supermarket ads across the country.

Who doesn't love to shop at a farmers' market? Although the prices aren't always cheaper, many of us find great value in buying fresh produce direct from local growers.

Supermarket produce could come from practically anywhere and it is often grown to withstand shipping long distances.

Although this is only a snapshot, it is comprehensive and countrywide. We felt it was the best, most reliable source for baseline pricing information.

We used the report for mid-July. Due to seasonality, several edibles on our master list were not included in the report. So in those instances where we needed a national average, echoing the method that the USDA uses, we did our own survey of supermarkets in different regions. These samplings included random supermarkets in the north, south, east, and west of the country.

Supermarkets Versus Farmers' Markets

But why supermarkets? Given the difference between the standardized and often processed nature of supermarket produce and what comes out of most backyard

GROWING VALUE: THE DIFFERENCE BEYOND DOLLARS

Even though the produce available in your local farmers' market may be pricier than what you find in the local supermarket, when it comes to assessing price-per-pound of any produce, you have to make sure that what you're comparing is, well, truly comparable. Studies from industry organizations, such as the Northeast Organic Farming Association's Vermont's Pricing Study, have found that on a pure calorie quality-to-price comparison, farmers' market produce is actually on par with the prices you'd find in supermarket.

There are other, less tangible benefits as well. A survey in *Farmers Markets Today* revealed that more than 85 percent of the produce in local farmers' markets traveled less than 50 miles to get to the market. Many farmers markets require that the produce sold be grown "locally," within a predetermined range (often as little as 10 miles from the market—they could walk it to market!). Obviously, the transport distance, and time from field to shelf, is far greater with supermarkets. That means more fuel burned and produce that ripens in

transit rather than on the plant. Given that studies have long shown that nutritional value in produce degrades over time, the price on that lug of tomatoes or a few ears of corn is only one—and perhaps not the best in every case—indicator of high value.

There are even more esoteric concerns that may appeal to one person or another on a personal level. Farmers' markets help support small family farms and are usually a way to keep money within a local community. The point is, garden investment is—to one degree or another—in the eye of the beholder.

---

gardens, there was an argument to be made for using produce prices from farmers' markets. Unfortunately, we not only could not find a reliable comprehensive database on farmers' market prices comparable to the USDA's National Retail Report, the sampling size would have been a whole lot smaller. The Farmers Market Directory available on the website of the industry group Farmers Market Coalition lists 8,100 registered markets in the 2013 directory. For that same year, the Food Marketing Institute listed over 37,000 supermarkets with $2 million or more in annual sales. That's almost a five-fold difference.

The differences in costs are going to be much greater among farmer's markets region to region, given the localized nature of farmers' costs and related expenses. For instance, the organizations that run local farmers' markets often charge fees. On the other hand, large supermarket chains often buy one type of produce from a single major farm supplier. The price of that item will vary little from store to store in the chain. The same is not true from farmers' market to farmers' market. Those variations are one more reason why we choose supermarkets for pricing information.

Accounting for Diversity

One of the biggest challenges in researching the price-per-pound category is making direct comparisons to individual classes of vegetables without considering the differences variety to variety. There is a limited amount of diversity in supermarket produce because the crops are chosen for qualities like durability and resistance to the stress of shipping. All that produce must also look uniform and capture what the average shopper has come to expect a potato, tomato, or head of Romaine lettuce is supposed to look like. Supermarkets are trying to give their customers what they want, not just what's available.

If you visit a farmers' market, you'll see greater diversity. Small farmers can afford to grow different varieties, including those less sensitive to the strains of transportation and corporate production. For instance, you're far more likely to find heirloom tomatoes in many sizes, colors, and textures (including what the average consumer might think is too soft) at a market or co-op than anything you would find in a supermarket.

We've attempted to account for the many variations among any given crop (i.e., we've included four different tomatoes in the calculations). As much as possible, distinct differences between widely available varieties are also dealt with in the text under each listing. This will be give you some direction in selecting, for example, the types of carrots or tomatoes you plant, and should help you balance that fine line between what you're most interested in growing, and which varieties or types will deliver the biggest return on investment.

Some rare exceptions exist. If you live in a state that doesn't grow a highly perishable crop, importing that crop could be expensive and will be reflected in your local costs. That will be something to consider when you're judging crops against each other and consulting the listings.

The part that may really amaze you is what the numbers work out to be. For instance, you might not think of plain old basil as a cash crop, but it turns out that

A tomato is not a tomato is not a tomato. We couldn't possibly treat each of the thousands of tomato varieties grown individually, so as with some other veggies we broke tomatoes down into categories for purposes of comparison: heirloom, hybrid, cherry, and Roma (determinate). You'll have to read on to find out which of the types has the best return on investment. (HINT: Sometimes big things come in little packages.)

the price per pound can run higher than $16. I've seen a lot of jaws drop when I tell gardeners that fact. But the math doesn't lie. Most basil offered at retail is sold in small plastic packages of two or three stems with mature leaves. The weight is often less than an ounce—and can cost $3 or $4! Imagine enough of that basil to make a pound. Then consider what a single, healthy, thriving basil plant will produce over a season. Suddenly, the big number makes sense.

The "Real" Price Per Pound

Ultimately, the important thing to note is that we've used the same pricing rationale for all the price-per-pound numbers in the listings. This gives you a starting point. You can refine the calculations to reflect your own garden's value based on whether you're growing produce that is closer to what you'll find in the local farmer's market, or more mainstream varieties that resembles what's on offer at the local supermarket. In most cases, the reality lies in the middle ground between those two prices.

LOCATION AND PRICE

The reason we used national average prices per pound for the listings in the vegetable calculations was because prices can vary significantly from one region of the country to another. This is more a consequence of shipping than of individual state economies.

Regionality will also affect the number of farmers' markets and co-ops in a given area. If you're lucky enough to have an abundance of these types of farm-to-table outlets, you may want to substitute the average prices we've used for the prices that are closer to what you'll find locally.

In any case, keep in mind that the variables we've included are flexible; adjust the figures as you see fit to reflect local conditions.

What a Difference a Year Makes

Nobody controls the weather, which is why there is no way to account for severe weather events in static calculations like those used in Section 2. As hurricanes, droughts, and other severe weather events become commonplace, agricultural production can vary wildly from one year to next. Changes in the weather may change the value outlook of whatever you decide to grow.

Water is an inescapable expense for just about every garden, and it's getting more costly all the time. You can limit water usage by practicing smart watering techniques: for plain efficiency, nothing is better than pouring water slowly right at the base of each plant so you're not watering any weeds or bare soil.

GARDEN CROP PRODUCTION COSTS

Many different variables go into growing a garden, involving a variety of expenses. The costs associated with gardening can be divided into two groups—what we'll call fixed costs, and ongoing expenses that you'll deal with in each growing season.

Generally, if you buy a quality garden trowel, it will last for a very long time and the cost will be amortized over the years, so that expense actually impacts your garden's overall financial picture very little. Something like water or seeds is an ongoing expense that is incurred each season. Ongoing costs have the biggest impact on your garden expenses and how much return on investment you realize from what you grow. Ongoing costs also rise over time.

Because both types of garden expenses change radically based on myriad factors—from the size of your garden, to what you grow, to the gardening method you're using—adding these expenses into the formula we used for our calculations didn't make sense. But that's not to say you should ignore them.

INVESTING IN GARDENING TOOLS

The best bargain in gardening tools is not always the cheapest option available. In a bottom-line sense, the best investment you can make is the tool that lasts the longest relative to its original cost. Here are some tool fine points that you should consider the next time you're shopping in the garden center:

- Comfort
- Durable materials
- Quality construction

No matter what tools you buy, you'll get the most value out of them by taking care of your tools during and after the season. Sharpen bladed tools prior to working with them to make the work easier and the tool last longer. Properly store hand tools on a peg rack or other unit that keeps them organized and off the garage or shed floor. At the end of the season, clean and store your gardening hand tools in a dry space that doesn't experience freezing temperatures or excessive condensation.

The number and type of tools you need to grow edibles depends a lot on the gardening method you choose. One of the great advantages of Square Foot Gardening is that you only need four tools: a trowel, a bucket, a pair of scissors (I like the cheap kids' style), and a pencil.

In looking at your own expenses and what you grow, you may want to keep track of significant costs. You can then choose to calculate them against the projected ROI from our listings for the crops you've grown. There's another reason to track costs as well: there are a number of strategies you can use to reduce those costs once you identify them.

Gardening Tools

Basic gardening requires few tools, and most of those implements are inexpensive. At the minimum you'll need a trowel and gardening gloves (for Square Foot Gardening and most container gardening). You may also need a garden spade, fork, cultivator, and hoe for more traditional gardening approaches. The reality is that these tools will usually last more than a decade with a minimum of care, and can easily be purchased used or on sale. Ultimately, if you spread the cost out over years of gardening, tool expenses will have little impact on the overall value of what you grow.

Equipment Issues

Garden value can also be affected by any equipment you'll need for the crops you raise, although this will generally be a much smaller expense than tools. You'll use your judgment as to whether to associate equipment cost with a single crop—and add it to the "input" amount for that crop in your calculations—or spread the cost of equipment across several or all of your crops.

Usually this is a fairly clear-cut issue. Cages or trellises for your tomato plants should be an expense added to the input costs for your tomatoes (after being divided by the number of years of life you expect to get out of the cage or trellis). The cost of something like lumber for raised beds should be divided evenly across all the crops grown in that bed (again, divided by the number of years you expect the wood to last).

But some expenses will be hard to calculate into any given crop. A new garden hose, for example, might be used for both your garden plants and a portion of your landscaping. A container bought for a container garden may be used for other plants in the future and could feasibly last so long as to represent a miniscule expense when the purchase price is divided over years of use. As far as I'm concerned, when in doubt, leave it out of the calculations.

The best part of taking a bottom-line approach to everything you buy for the garden is that you quickly see how expenses can add up. I think a big part of high-value gardening—one that is easily overlooked—is cutting down on these incidental equipment expenses. The best way to do that is to find items to reuse and recycle in place of garden equipment. An existing cyclone fence can be a trellis. And if you're looking to build raised beds, you can often find free lumber from construction sites. (Just be sure and always ask before taking anything from a work site, and never use treated wood or any that has been painted.)

Adding Amendments

You'll quickly notice in reviewing the calculations that we've left out any numbers for the cost of fertilizer, compost, plant food, bone meal, and other amendments. Frankly there's little that is constant among amendments. Depending on the makeup of your soil (how rich it is, how well it drains, etc.) you may need far fewer amendments than a person in the next town over. You may, in fact, need none. If you're growing in a Square Foot Garden, you don't need to add anything once you've created the ideal growing medium I call "Mel's Mix." It's equal parts peat moss, vermiculite, and blended compost. You can also limit your input expense by choosing to grow vegetables and varieties known for their hardiness and ability to make do with fewer nutrients and water than other plants.

Wherever they are growing, plants do best in rich, nutritious soil that drains well. Creating that situation is a garden-wide issue—you don't just improve the area where your tomato plants will grow. That means that any significant soil amendment expenses would take an equal bite out of the return on investment from all the plants you grow.

COMPOST

Composting is one of the biggest favors you can do for your garden, your wallet, and the environment at large. Everything from eggshells to fall leaves, grass clippings, kitchen waste, and even unfinished cardboard boxes can be composted. The process is easy, takes little time and effort, and provides a rich improvement to the nutrition and texture of your soil. Although you can buy compost made from different source materials, general compost from a backyard composting bin or pile is usually just as good and costs you nothing.

Creating your own compost in a compost bin is a great way to save money, and it has real benefits for the environment, too. And plants love it. For making Mel's Mix, I like to blend many types, including some bagged products, but the best is still the compost you make yourself.

Priceless H$_2$O

Water is increasingly becoming a scarce commodity in areas across the country. The result is that local water companies are creating thresholds. Once exceeded, the cost of water doubles or triples. This presents a challenge to anyone looking to grow a large and varied garden. Given how much water any garden plot can consume, we had a discussion about including water usage in the expenses calculated against crop yield value, but that was problematic. Depending on where you live in the country, your water bill may range from eye-popping to insignificant. Water usage is also rarely broken down into inside and outside the house, so a high water bill may reflect long showers and frequent clothes washer and dishwasher use every bit as much as watering your garden.

But there's no getting around the fact that certain plants are thirstier than others. If you live in an area of the country regularly affected by drought, such as central California, there is a good case to be made for adjusting the overall ROI calculations of all your crops by a percentage of your water bill. No matter what, to maintain maximum garden value, take steps to limit your outside water use.

Free water! Install a rain barrel or two to put that free water from the sky to good use (and keep it out of the sewer system).

- Water in the early morning or early evening to avoid excessive evaporation.

- Collect water if possible. A rainwater collection system is a good way to supplement city or well water, especially for watering crops. Specialized greywater systems may also work if they recycle water from low-impact sources such as the kitchen sink. However, check local codes for regulations concerning greywater usage and edible plants.

- Mulch wherever it won't impact the health of your edible plants. A layer of mulch at least 4 inches thick will go a long way toward conserving soil moisture.

- Use a drip irrigation system rather than a sprinkler or hose. A sprinkler will moisten leaves which can, on many plants, lead to disease. Using a sprinkler also results in a vast amount of water lost to evaporation. A hose supplies so much water so quickly that much of it simply drains away. You can also water by hand if that is a practical option given the size of your garden and the amount of time you're willing or able to dedicate to it.

Labor Costs

The calculations for Section 2's listings could have included some factor that accounted for gardening labor, but in the end we chose to leave that out for three reasons. First, everybody puts a different value on his or her own labor. Does a doctor's time spent in the garden have more value than time spent by someone earning minimum wage? Who's to say what per-hour rate would be appropriate? Second, the amount of labor you put in changes depending on how much you grow and how you grow—what type of gardening you do. For instance, raised bed

GROWING VALUE: 5 BEST DROUGHT-TOLERANT VEGETABLES

You can conserve water by choosing your vegetable garden plants carefully. Some are naturally better suited to thriving under the pressure of restricted water, and others simply don't need plentiful moisture. As a rule of thumb, edible plants and varieties with smaller leaves and smaller fruits generally use less water.

1 **HOT PEPPER**
2 **ROSEMARY**
3 **OKRA**
4 **GARLIC**
5 **BEAN (POLE AND BUSH)**

gardening takes more time and effort up front, but is usually less labor intensive as the growing season progresses. Third, and perhaps most importantly, I've always felt that gardening was enjoyable time well spent. Most gardeners I've worked with or talked to agree. It's a wonderful opportunity to get some practical exercise, enjoy fresh air and sunshine, and get away from pressures in your life. Like a lot of people, the joy I get from gardening can't be calculated like work. In the end, if you must, go ahead and add a per-hour rate broken down across the season and across all the plants you grow. But be prepared that the figure will most likely skew your return on investment into the negative numbers.

The Cost of Land

Although gardeners rarely think of it this way, land can be considered a gardening expense. Committing a portion of your backyard—or front yard—to a garden (even a Square Foot Garden) means not using that portion for recreation, landscaping for property value, or some other use. However, garden land value is an esoteric calculation and one that most people would agree should not have a direct impact on the value of produce grown on your property.

A fee-based community garden or rental plot is another case entirely. If you are paying for access to the plot where you set up your garden, it only makes sense to divide the total outlay across the input calculations for all your crops. This can be a handy catch-all expense, because fee-for-planting community garden plots often include water and even amendments within the fee.

The Starting Point

Just about every plant can be started from seed, but in a home garden, many are often planted as "starts" of one sort or another—seedlings, cuttings, or bulblets. Take asparagus. Asparagus is normally purchased and planted as crowns. I've kept this in mind throughout the calculations; where the crop is most commonly planted as a seed, the input for that crop will be the seed packet price, divided by the number of seeds in a packet, and then multiplied by the number recommended by the seed company for planting a square foot. If the crop is conventionally planted as starts, I've used the cost-per-start based on an average of nursery prices, multiplied by the number of starts that would be planted in a square foot.

Using seed prices as a one-time expense can be a little trickier than just plugging a number into a simple formula. Some plants, such as the asparagus mentioned above, grow as perennials (and asparagus won't produce a crop for two years unless you buy mature crowns). Buy them once and the plant will produce for years. Other crops, such as carrots, require new seeds every season. To deal with this, I've divided the seed prices in half for any plant that can grow more than one year. This is a conservative estimate, meaning these plants will probably have a real-world return on investment even higher than what is recorded in the listing.

Whether to grow from seeds planted directly into your garden, seeds started indoors, or purchased seedlings is a major decision that will have a great impact on the ROI of any crop you grow.

It should be pretty easy to see that this is one of the more complicated columns to fill out on the chart. This is where you could theoretically calculate in water costs, fertilizer, mulch, topsoil, equipment, and other expenses. Certainly, many articles about determining the dollar value of a garden suggest doing just that. To me, these are total gardening expenses. You can always handicap one of the listings if you think that particular crop is going to take up more than its fair share of resources in your garden. But I've tried to keep the calculations included in the Section 2 listings as simple and direct as possible. You can consider them a starting point, off of which you can build as you see fit.

HIGH-VALUE VEGGIES:
THE WINNERS!

And now, the moment you've all been waiting for. The envelope please…and the homegrown edible with the highest return on investment is…herbs! The runner up: parsnip. And in third place: cherry tomato.

Our congratulations to the winners! And now that the suspense is over, here's the whole story.

The listings that follow describe all 59 edible plants we looked at in this little competition. Herbs (we included twelve different ones) came up so high because of their relative price-per-pound at retail, that we made the decision to separate them out and award first place to the entire category, even though, as you'll see, the actual ROI does vary among specific herbs. Consequently, the listings begin with the "Herb" section and the herbs in descending order of ROI. Then we move onto the vegetables and present them in order of ranking from highest to lowest ROI.

WHAT DO WE MEAN BY VALUE?

As we talked about a little earlier, value means many things to many people. Our winner is based on a cold, analytical evaluation of return on investment. That may sound a bit harsh when you're talking about yummy, beautiful produce that's made from seeds, water, and sunshine. But if you're trying to decide what's worth growing in your own garden, it's important. For a fascinating look at some other ways to consider value, don't miss the listings in Section 3, starting on page 94.

HIGH-VALUE VEGGIES:
MEL'S TOP TEN

The list of high-value garden winners features some surprises, such as a not-widely-loved root that perhaps should get more attention than it does. There are also some edibles on the list that should surprise no one: tomatoes remain both a popular vegetable and a solid garden investment.

1 HERBS

The high-value powerhouses overwhelmed the vegetables when it comes to ROI. The ones we included in this general category are (in order of ROI): thyme, rosemary, mint, chives, tarragon, basil, oregano, dill, sage, cilantro, Italian parsley, and curly parsley.

2 PARSNIP

Not familiar with this easy-to-grow root? You should be. Offering enviable nutrition and fiber, the lowly parsnip makes a wonderful, lower-starch alternative to mashed potatoes, and needs only a little dressing up with some butter, pepper, and kiss of Parmesan cheese. One bite and you're sure to find a place in your garden for this top performer.

3 CHERRY TOMATO

The combination of small, bite-sized fruit and prolific production in a small area combined to land this lovely vegetable garden addition high on the list. Perfect for containers, raised beds, and traditional gardens alike, this is a star performer.

4 GARLIC

Garlic can be crowded and still do well. The production in a square foot accounts for the bulbous vegetable's prize mid-list position, and the fact that garlic can easily be stored for months only adds to its appeal.

5 HEIRLOOM TOMATO

Unusual and unique, with distinctively rich and deep flavors, heirloom tomatoes are quickly becoming a favorite type to include in larger gardens and anywhere eaters don't mind odd shapes, colors, patterns, and sizes in their tomatoes. This delicious edible bought its way onto the high-value list because they are so expensive at retail—but that doesn't mean they are any harder to grow than hybrids!

6 TURNIP

Yet another root vegetable that made the Top 10. This one is a sleeper that boasts not just a richly flavored root, but super nutritious greens as well. Many cooks combine the two for stunning vegetarian dishes—the root is as good in soups as it is roasted. All that, and turnips are easy to grow. A miniature variety called 'Japanese Turnips' is harvested when it's about the size of a large radish. They grow fast, and are very pretty. I've used these to encourage kids to eat something besides fries!

7 LEEK

Boasting a distinctive flavor a cut above the common onion, leeks are fairly simple to grow and require only ample water and nutrition to thrive. The sheer weight of the harvest accounts for its high position on the list, but if culinary potential had been factored in, it might have been even higher up.

8 WINTER SQUASH

This is one of the most surprising crops among the top 10, but winter squash earned its position with the sheer yield. That means, in the most practical sense, winter squashes of all types produce a ton of usable calories. And that's not all. These odd-shaped vegetables provide a wealth of nutrients and a high amount of fiber, which spells health no matter what rank it's given.

9 SPINACH

The calculations favored the productivity of spinach plants against a relatively high retail price among all greens. But what's not counted in the calculations are the vitamins and minerals spinach offers. You might also consider harvesting the leaves early because baby spinach leaves are especially tender and flavorful—perfect for when you're eating the vegetable raw.

10 HYBRID TOMATO

Rounding out the three types of tomatoes in the top ten, this is the most common. But even within hybrid varieties, you'll find a lot of diversity from which to choose. Tomatoes of all kinds remain a favorite among gardeners everywhere for the delicious, abundant fruit.

MEL'S BOTTOM TEN

It's important to note that just because a crop falls to the bottom of this list, it shouldn't be dismissed out of hand. Financially, these are the vegetables that make the least sense to grow, but there are lots of other reasons to pick one crop over another. For instance, several of these can be considered "superfoods" crammed full of nutrients. Or perhaps you just love a nice, crisp homegrown potato (I know I do), in which case you probably don't care that they finished dead last in our high-value survey.

1	**POTATO**	Much beloved, but potatoes simply don't produce enough yield to combat a very low price in the supermarket. Still, it is one of the more fun crops to grow and certainly one of the most delicious. To be honest, I was a bit surprised they came in last place in our ROI rankings. Sorry, spuds.
2	**BRUSSELS SPROUTS**	Wonderful cancer-fighting compounds and a well-rounded flavor point to a better position on the list for Brussels sprouts. The story here, though, is one of production. The yield is too modest to make a big profit from the supermarket price per pound.
3	**BELL PEPPER**	Who would have guessed? As popular as bell peppers are for the sweet flavor and beautiful colors, this is one of the most widely available—and inexpensive—vegetables in the supermarket produce aisle. The plants are also not as prolific as other contenders.
4	**SWISS CHARD**	This is the big surprise in the bottom ten. Delicious and incredibly nutritious, Swiss chard is also one of the most beautiful greens you can put on the table. But a low retail price point, and modest yield weight, translated to a low ranking.
5	**ASPARAGUS**	The initial expense, difficulty of cultivation, long maturation, and relatively low retail price point all combine to lower this popular and tasty spear vegetable down to the bottom. But to those who love the flavor and culinary adaptability of this gem, the low ranking is not well deserved.
6	**OKRA**	The low ranking reflects okra's lack of wide popularity (unless you live in the South) and the modest price at retail. It is an acquired taste, and one that cannot compete on a broad list of vegetables such as this.
7&8	**BEAN (POLE & BUSH)**	Beans are an example of a modest financial performer that remains a popular backyard garden crop. A low retail price despite a good yield accounts for the bottom-of-list placement, but this is still a fun vegetable for kids, and a highly nutritious garden addition. Another nice thing about beans is that you can grow different varieties either low as bush beans or high as pole beans.
9	**CELERY**	Although this salad ingredient is fairly easy to grow, the low ranking is a consequence of low retail pricing due to the unexciting nature of the vegetable. It can be used in many ways in the kitchen, but doesn't provide the flavor explosion of others on this list.
10	**GREEN CABBAGE**	Rounding out the list, the 10th-lowest ROI veggie is green cabbage. It takes a lot to grow this highly nutritious and cancer-fighting vegetable. Between a lengthy growing period and the large space a single head requires, the return on investment is low. But you would be hard pressed to find a green more adaptable in the kitchen and more chock full of vitamins and nutrients.

HIGH-VALUE VEGGIES:
MEL'S COMPLETE LIST

	VEGGIE	ROI*
1	HERBS (THYME)	$69.08
2	PARSNIP	$35.04
3	TOMATO, CHERRY	$26.13
4	GARLIC	$25.21
5	TOMATO, HEIRLOOM	$23.65
6	TURNIP	$22.86
7	LEEK	$18.72
8	SQUASH, WINTER	$18.15
9	SPINACH	$16.54
10	TOMATO, HYBRID	$16.13
11	MUSTARD GREENS	$13.90
12	ONION, YELLOW	$12.00
13	PUMPKIN	$11.76
14	LETTUCE, MESCLUN	$11.62
15	ARUGULA	$11.01
16	CUCUMBER	$10.71
17	LETTUCE, ROMAINE	$10.62
18	ONION, WHITE	$9.16
19	TOMATO, ROMA	$7.97
20	ONION, RED	$7.71
21	WATERMELON	$7.71
22	LETTUCE, GREEN/RED LEAF	$7.54
23	STRAWBERRY	$7.45
24	ZUCCHINI, SUMMER SQUASH	$6.80
25	LETTUCE, BUTTER	$5.81
26	RADICCHIO	$5.79
27	KOHLRABI	$5.40
28	FENNEL (BULB)	$4.74
29	EGGPLANT	$4.45
30	CANTALOUPE (MUSKMELON)	$3.96

	VEGGIE	ROI*
31	CARROT, HEIRLOOM	$3.45
32	RADISH, DAIKON	$3.36
33	COLLARD GREENS	$3.19
34	CORN	$2.87
35	CABBAGE, SAVOY	$2.85
36	BROCCOLI	$2.76
37	CABBAGE, NAPA	$2.18
38	PEA, SUGAR SNAP	$1.80
39	CARROT, HYBRID	$1.73
40	KALE	$1.02
41	PEA, SNOW	$1.02
42	RADISH	$1.02
43	BEET	$1.01
44	ARTICHOKE	$0.81
45	CAULIFLOWER	$0.75
46	CABBAGE, RED	$0.63
47	SWEET POTATO	$0.62
48	CABBAGE, GREEN	$0.60
49	CELERY	$0.55
50	BEAN, BUSH	-$0.11
51	BEAN, POLE	-$0.40
52	OKRA	-$0.70
53	ASPARAGUS	-$0.90
54	SWISS CHARD	-$1.62
55	BELL PEPPER	-$1.90
56	BRUSSELS SPROUTS	-$3.81
57	POTATO, RUSSET	-$4.38
58	POTATO, YELLOW	-$5.96
59	POTATO, RED	-$6.22

*ROI = Return on investment per square foot planted

THE WINNER: HERBS

The profiles in this section are brief snapshots of each edible's characteristics, relevant tips, and information about how to get the best yield (and the best value) out of each plant, and other insights. In most cases, if you're unfamiliar with the cultivation of any of these, it's wisest to round out your knowledge by consulting a nursery pro or researching a little bit to ensure that you get the best value. Losing a season's worth of any crop due to a lack of knowledge is the opposite of high value.

Where they were particularly relevant, I've included some examples of specific varieties you might want to consider for one reason or another. Here again, these are merely suggestions, offered as a starting point for making your own garden plan. You'll have to decide for yourself what the most important features of your edible garden plants are—gross yield, culinary potential, disease and pest resistance, enchanting appearance, or a combination of two or more of these.

I've also included a feature called "Value Added" where I break down key points relating to getting the best value possible out of each individual crop. If you really are dedicated to achieving the highest return on investment for what you plant and cultivate in your edible garden, this is the type of thinking you should always be doing when considering the garden.

The lovely herbs you'll see on the next few pages don't represent an exhaustive list of all the herbs you can grow, but they do represent the herbs that are most commonly sold and consumed. Given their high overall rankings, it might make the most sense to grow a collection as a kitchen garden (depending on how much you cook—most of these are most effective when combined in prepared dishes with other more central ingredients).

Herbs like these make an excellent mixed garden, especially when you mix in a small number of edible flowers (see page 116). That can be a great way to keep an eye on your investment in herbs.

Wherever you plant them, keep in mind that some are perennials and some are annuals. Almost all of these love sun and will grow well in containers. Before you decide how many plants of your favorite herb to cultivate, realistically assess just how much of the herb you will use over the season and how well any unused portions will freeze or can be dried. Then plan and plant accordingly. Growing just the right amount of herbs is crucial to optimizing your garden investment.

The winner's bouquet: Why not make it with herbs? Shown here are parsley, basil, rosemary, thyme, and sage (if you look closely, you'll spot some marjoram too). Not pictured here: mint, chives, French tarragon, oregano, dill, sage, cilantro, and parsley.

HERBS, THYME

Thyme is a plant-anywhere herb that fits in wherever you might put it in your garden or landscape. A wonderful fragrant groundcover, it can also serve as a spreading, low-lying groundcover. The miniature purple-pink flowers are a delight, and the smell is simply inviting.

As with all herbs, thyme needs well-drained soil to thrive (even if it is in sandy or other less-than-perfectly nutritious soils). Hailing from the Mediterranean, thyme does best in full sun and slightly alkaline soil. It will behave as a perennial in many zones, but will die under the extreme heat of southern regions in Zones 7 and up. Lemon thyme, however, can survive hotter areas and is a hardier variety in general.

The most reliable way to plant thyme is by using starts, because seeds are unreliable. Mulch around new plantings to prevent weeds, which are competitors to thyme seedlings. After the plants become established, thyme requires very little care. The most flavorful leaves will be harvested before the plant flowers in mid summer, but you can continue harvesting leaves as needed into winter.

In spring, cut back woody and dead growth to the closest new growth on the stems. Thyme can also be dried by hanging sprigs, tied together, in a warm, dry, well-ventilated space. Store them in an airtight container. If you prefer a quicker preservation method, you can freeze sprigs in a resealable bag, but drying intensifies the herb's flavor.

NAME:	Thyme, #1 Herbs
YIELD/FOOT (LB.)	2.00
COST/LB.	$42.44
VALUE	$84.88
INPUT	$15.80
ROI	$69.08
ROI%	437%

Value Added:
- Thyme is an excellent companion to cabbage and broccoli. Plant it next to or around those vegetables to deter whitefly infestations.

HERBS, ROSEMARY

This perennial is one of the most durable and productive herbs. It is amazingly easy to grow and adds a distinctive and appealing flavor to anything it touches, from grilled veggies to roasted lamb to flavored oils.

Rosemary doesn't need particularly rich soil to thrive; any area in the garden that receives full sun and good air circulation will do. Rosemary also makes a great container plant on a sunny deck or patio. This is not an ideal option for colder northern zones (severe winters with temperatures that consistently fall below freezing) where the herb will need to be taken inside to overwinter.

Plant rosemary by seed, and water well as it grows, allowing the soil to dry out between waterings. Keep an eye out for signs of powdery mildew—one of the few conditions that can attack the plant. Cut out any affected area. Insects and wildlife generally leave rosemary plants alone.

If you're mulching around a rosemary plant to keep down weeds or retain soil moisture, make sure there is space between the plant's root crown and the mulch. Prune out dead wood in spring to keep the plant looking sharp and thriving.

Harvest a sprig at any time, cutting the woody stems cleanly with pruning shears. You can also cut several sprigs and dry them upside down, for the less-intense flavor of the dried herb.

Value Added:

- Rosemary's value isn't limited to the kitchen. This is an exceptional filler plant for rock gardens, and shines when planted as a tumbling hedge next to a garden pathway. When a visitor walks by, the subtle pine scent makes the stroll evocative and raises the appetite.

NAME:	Rosemary, #1 Herbs
YIELD/FOOT (LB.)	1.00
COST/LB.	$42.44
VALUE	$42.44
INPUT	$0.01
ROI	$42.43
ROI%	424,300%

HERBS, MINT

It's easy to fall in love with the appealing fragrance and lovely flavor of mint, but temper your affection. This is an aggressive, prolific perennial. A single plant often supplies much more fresh mint than a family of four can use. That's why we recommend you grow it in a container all by itself.

Choose the type of mint carefully. Sweet mint is the most common for home gardeners, but you can opt for bracing spearmint, the fun and curative peppermint, or the unusual chocolate mint.

Mint grows easily in partial shade and damp conditions, so it may be a good candidate for that corner of the garden other plants don't like. It is also an attractive ornamental filler, and a fantastic performer in containers. You can even use it as groundcover between pavers.

The key to success lies in protecting the young plants, which are susceptible to attack from a number of small insects such as spider mites. Watch them closely and use insecticidal soap as necessary.

Harvest the leaves as you need them by simply pinching off the stems. You can take a large yield from the plant when mature, especially right before it flowers, when the flavor is especially intense.

Value Added:
- Make the most of the mint you grow by using it in interesting dishes for dinner and beyond. Mint can replace or supplement herbal ingredients, such as the basil in pesto, or it can be used as a key flavor in Mediterranean and Middle Eastern dishes. Take the opportunity of a mint crop to expand your cooking repertoire.

NAME:	Mint, #1 Herbs
YIELD/FOOT (LB.)	1.00
COST/LB.	$42.44
VALUE	$42.44
INPUT	$0.03
ROI	$42.41
ROI%	141,367%

HERBS, CHIVES

Not only do chives supply a subtle, delectable onion flavor, but the plant also produces showcase purple blooms when allowed to flower. They are so easy to grow that there really is no reason not to set aside a little room for at least a small harvest.

The plant does best in full sun but will tolerate partial shade and will even grow in marginally nutritious soil.

However, chives are occasionally susceptible to soil and leaf diseases like mold and rust. Keep your chives healthy with proper soil hygiene, careful watering, and good air circulation.

Although the harvest may seem modest, this plant is actually a giver. After the first frost in the fall, cut the plant back to a clump and it will grow again the following spring. Chive plants can produce for several years. Although the flowers are quite beautiful, pinch them off if you want to increase your harvest of leaves.

Value Added:

- Get the best value by using all parts of a chive plant. The flowers are edible with a pronounced onion flavor. They make stunning additions to a garden salad, and can even be used as garnish with beef, pork, and chicken dishes.

- Don't waste any of your chive harvest. Fresh chives that you won't use in a few days can be frozen in plastic resealable bags, or chopped up and dried. Dried chives have a much less potent flavor and can replace fresh chives in a recipe when used two-for-one.

- Double down on your investment by dividing your plants every three years to cultivate free new chive plants and boost the production of existing plants.

NAME:	Chives, #1 Herbs
YIELD/FOOT (LB.)	1.00
COST/LB.	$42.40
VALUE	$42.40
INPUT	$0.99
ROI	$41.41
ROI%	4,183%

HERBS, FRENCH TARRAGON

Boasting the beauty of an ornamental grass and an elegant licorice flavor, French tarragon is one of the most underappreciated herbs in America's kitchen gardens.

The plant does not usually flower and rarely produces seeds, which means you'll be planting a seedling from a root cutting (unless you take a root cutting yourself). The herb does best in zones where both summer and winter are mild. In those regions, it will grow as a perennial. In hotter parts of the country, it's planted as an annual.

French tarragon can endure drought, but will not thrive in waterlogged soil. Make sure the bed drains well, even if the soil occasionally goes dry. The plant may look like it's dying in winter, but be patient. Cut back brown and dead growth in early spring, and the plant is likely to come back in full force.

You can harvest individual leaves as needed. A little bit goes a long way in the kitchen, so the entire plant is almost never cut down. The herb is most often used fresh in recipes, although you can freeze it for later use, by putting sprigs in a resealable plastic bag and freezing them. Unfortunately, tarragon loses its flavor when dried.

NAME:	French Tarragon, #1 Herbs			
YIELD/FOOT (LB.)	1.00			
COST/LB.	$42.44			
VALUE	$42.44			
INPUT	$6.34			
ROI	$36.10			
ROI%	569%			

Value Added:

- If French tarragon thrives in your garden, you can realize more value from the plant by dividing it every third year.

- The trick to growing this sophisticated herb is finding ways to use the harvest. French cooks put it into sauces, dressings, stews and use it as a coating for roasted chicken. Plant French tarragon as a way to spur experimentation and broaden your dinner menus.

HERBS, BASIL

Most gardeners find that there is no such thing as too much basil. The herb is used in a wide range of cuisines, from Italian and Greek to Asian. It's also fairly expensive at retail, making this a wonderful high-value crop for your kitchen garden, container garden, or veggie bed.

Basil grows easily in the soil or in containers and is usually only bothered by slugs, aphids, or Japanese beetles, all of which are easy to eradicate. Keep the soil just moist—dry soil can stunt the plants. Basil should produce until the first frost; cold weather quickly kills the plant, although you can bring it indoors near a sunny window for a slightly extended season.

The most common Genovese basil is not the only variety; you can also grow purple or Thai basil for a slightly different flavor and a very different look in the garden. Basil is often used as an addition to an ornamental kitchen garden because it is attractive. Consider 'African Blue', the large-leafed 'Green Ruffles', the unusual flavor of lemon basil, or distinctively spicy leaves and flowers of 'Spicy Globe'.

Value Added:

- Pinch back basil stem tips to prevent the plants from flowering and to make them grow bushier.

- When basil plants bolt, use the flowers in the kitchen to get the best value from the plant. They can be chopped and sprinkled on salads, and are absolutely heavenly when breaded and fried!

- Get more from your plants by using them as decoration in terra cotta pots right outside your kitchen door.

NAME:	Basil, #1 Herbs
YIELD/FOOT (LB.)	0.50
COST/LB.	$64.72
VALUE	$32.36
INPUT	$0.21
ROI	$32.15
ROI%	15,310%

HERBS, OREGANO

This trouble-free herb grows like a weed, but it is the leaves' savory-sweet flavor and unforgettably delicious scent that makes it a must-have for the kitchen garden. European cooks have known this for centuries, and it accounts for this perennial's Mediterranean pedigree.

The plant is aggressive and spreading, so it is often grown in a container. Provide it healthy soil to start, and there will be no need for fertilizer during the season. Oregano is also usually pest and disease free, especially in a diverse garden where there are other plants to draw insects.

The flavor of the fresh herb will be most intense about mid summer, when flower buds have just formed, but are not yet opening. That said, you can cut leaf clusters any time after the plant reaches 8 inches tall. Cut stems back to a pair of leaves, and new branches will form from that spot.

Oregano can be used fresh or frozen for use in recipes later (in either case, the flavor fades quickly under heat, so add it only at the end of cooking). You can also dry your oregano—it's one of the few herbs with a more intense flavor when dried.

NAME:	Oregano, #1 Herbs
YIELD/FOOT (LB.)	0.75
COST/LB.	$42.44
VALUE	$31.83
INPUT	$0.04
ROI	$31.79
ROI%	79,479%

Value Added:

- Do not endanger your investment with water. Keep in mind that this is a Mediterranean plant. Water once a week and keep the soil fairly dry, because too much moisture will lead to root rot.

- Get double the bang for your buck by using oregano as a scented ornamental trailing or groundcover plant.

HERBS, DILL

Like many herbs, dill offers more than just a nice flavoring for many different recipes. It grows lace-like edible fronds and yellow flowers that are often used in bouquets. Dill is even planted as part of bushy, overflowing window boxes.

The plants can tolerate heat, but need steady, abundant water to thrive over hotter months. Heat considerations aside, the plant must absolutely have a maximum of direct sun during the day to ensure its base fills out and the plant grows as big a harvest as possible. Harvest the dill fresh by cutting the outer leaves close to the stem.

Cut flowers to encourage bushy growth. At the end of the season, let the plant bloom. Stake tall flower stems and you'll attract butterflies when the plant flowers. In fact, although the plants are susceptible to attack by parsleyworm caterpillar, many gardeners plant extra to accommodate any infestation because the caterpillars become stunning black butterflies.

Value Added:

- Letting this herb flower and bolt is the best way to get the most out of the plant in your garden. Cut off and dry the flowers and collect the seeds, which can be used as a flavorful savory spice in cooking. Dry the seedheads in a paper bag perforated with air holes, and then shake the seeds in the bag to separate them from the heads. Separate the seeds from the chaff by spreading them on a clean worktable and blowing a fan very softly across them. The lighter chaff will float away.

NAME:	Dill, #1 Herbs
YIELD/FOOT (LB.)	0.50
COST/LB.	$49.00
VALUE	$24.50
INPUT	$0.06
ROI	$24.44
ROI%	40,733%

HERBS, SAGE

Sage does quite well in containers and in garden beds. Its deep savory flavor inspires gardeners and cooks alike. Both the leaves and the flowers are excellent in a range of cold and hot dishes.

The herb is a perennial in all but the hottest, most humid parts of the country and the coldest regions. It cannot survive excessively high heat or consistently high humidity.

The most efficient way to start sage is as a cutting from an established plant or a nursery-bought seedling. Sage should be planted in soil with superior drainage, although it doesn't need to be overly nutritious. In fact, if the soil is too rich, the sage will grow leggy and tend to flop over, rather than growing in a nice, full, bushy mound. Once established as perennials, sage plants should be divided when they overgrow their beds or containers. Prune older plants in early spring to remove woodier old growth and encourage tender new growth.

Sage flowers in late summer or fall, and the blooms are both strikingly beautiful and edible.

NAME:	Sage, #1 Herbs		
YIELD/FOOT (LB.)	0.50		
COST/LB.	$42.44		
VALUE	$21.22		
INPUT	$0.25		
ROI	$20.97		
ROI%	8,388%		

Value Added:

- Although you can harvest individual leaves at any time, it's wise to harvest lightly in the first year, if you believe the sage will survive as a perennial in your region. Cutting stems modestly will ensure a nice full growth in the second year and up the overall value amortized over time.

HERBS, CILANTRO

Cilantro is a widely used herb, central to cuisines from the Middle East to South America. The unique, strong flavor can be overpowering, so one plant will usually fill the home cook's needs.

This is a fast-growing, cool-weather plant that does best in spring and fall, and will grow throughout mild summer temperatures. However, when the thermometer rises past 75 degrees Fahrenheit, it won't be long until the plant bolts, sending up lacy white flowers. Unlike other herbs, cilantro will not stop bolting merely because you pinch off the flower heads. You can buy bolt-resistant varieties if early bolting is a concern. Also called coriander, choose 'Calypso' for the traditional flavor and a pretty, lacy appearance, or 'Confetti' for a more unconventional, variegated, and rosemary-like appearance.

Cilantro requires a once-a-week watering and a little shelter from harsh winds. Otherwise, it is largely pest and disease resistant. However, cilantro plants do not like humid, rainy weather, and will not thrive in that condition.

Anytime after the plant reaches 6 inches tall, cut up to one-third at any one time. Leave it in place and let it grow into late fall, and it will reseed for a crop in spring.

Value Added:

- Get a two-for-one return on your cilantro investment by cultivating the coriander seeds from the seed heads once the plant bolts. The seeds are a spice used in many ethnic recipes. Let the seed heads brown, and then clip them and place them upside down in a paper bag. Within two or three days, the heads will split and drop the seeds.

NAME:	Cilantro, #1 Herbs
YIELD/FOOT (LB.)	1.00
COST/LB.	$3.12
VALUE	$3.12
INPUT	$0.12
ROI	$3.00
ROI%	2,500%

HERBS, PARSLEY

This is yet another easy herb to grow, one that is rarely bothered by pests or diseases and is prolific—you'll likely have more than you can use in a season. You'll choose between flat-leaf varieties (sometimes called Italian parsley) and curly. The flat-leaf is the choice of cooks for its superior flavor.

The calculations here include seedlings rather than seeds, because seeds take a long time to germinate and can be difficult to start indoors or allow for enough time to germinate in the ground.

Parsley does best planted in early spring, about a month before the last frost. Curly varieties will bolt under intense summer heat, but flat-leaved varieties are more heat tolerant and will last longer into the summer. In any case, do not let the soil completely dry out. If the parsley goes thirsty, the leaves will grow tough and bitter and be of little use in the kitchen.

You can take a small or large harvest from the plant, as soon as it reaches 5 inches or more. Cut off a small handful of outer leaves as needed or, if you need a larger amount, you can shear the whole plant back and it will quickly regrow.

Value Added:
- This is another herb that can bring just as much value to your garden design as it can to your kitchen. Curly varieties are excellent lush filler for window boxes, cut flower gardens, and decorative borders. Flat-leaf varieties are ideal as bushy green in amongst the stems and blooms of an edible flower garden.

NAME:	Flat-leaf, #1 Herbs	Curly, #1 Herbs
YIELD/FOOT (LB.)	0.75	0.75
COST/LB.	$7.62	$5.72
VALUE	$5.72	$4.29
INPUT	$4.00	$4.00
ROI	$1.72	$0.29
ROI%	43%	7%

Fresh vegetables are the reason for vegetable gardens, after all. The list of veggies with the highest return on investment contains some surprises.

AND NOW FOR THE VEGETABLES

Although they took a bit of a beating at the hands of the herbs value-wise, the real stars of most edible gardens are vegetables. So let's keep our high-ROI list moving with the veggies.

One of the things I love about working with numbers is they often surprise you. They can also be fun! (Bet you never thought that when you were sitting in math class.) The numbers that set the order of our list of vegetables revealed a fair share of surprises and some conclusions.

We started with the list itself. We included the most common fruits and vegetables that are grown in a garden. We naturally excluded trees and shrubs. An apple tree or a blackberry bramble are much greater commitments of time and resources, and are different from what most people would think of as belonging in a backyard garden.

We also didn't delve into individual varieties in the list. Varieties are a matter of preference. For annual fruits and vegetables, different varieties offer gardeners a chance to experiment. Plus, remember we were looking for standardization as much as possible. That said, we've included information on certain popular or standout varieties in some of the individual profiles of each crop that follow the top-to-bottom value listing.

The individual crops were ranked based on return on investment dollars. We felt that basing the rankings on dollars rather than the return-on-investment percentage (which we've also included) made more sense because it was most applicable in the real world. For your convenience, the rankings are also listed alphabetically on page 93.

PARSNIP

Parsnips are the woodier cousin to carrots. Shaped like a carrot, this root vegetable features a more complex, spiced sweetness and coarser, tougher texture. But parsnips make a wonderful addition to a collection of roasted vegetables or pureed as a substitute for mashed potatoes. They are also easy to grow and relatively trouble free.

The thing that parsnips must have—just as with other root vegetables—is well-turned, loose, quick-draining, and nutritious soil. Plant seeds in the garden in early spring, right after the last frost. The vegetable takes a long time to mature—four months or more. Fortunately, even if it's left in the ground when frost hits, it will be fine. In fact, the flavor is sweeter after a frost.

Parsnips are rarely attacked by pests and are little troubled by disease. If you suspect your garden harbors carrot rust flies, use a row cover over the new plants as they emerge. Harvest the roots as you would carrots, once the tops begin pushing out of the ground. You can even overwinter the crop by mulching over them with several inches of straw or similar mulch. Simply dig them up throughout winter and early spring. The greens are edible but not especially tasty. Most gardeners compost them.

Value Added:

- You'll give your parsnips the best possible chance by starting with the freshest seeds you can buy. Look at the date on the packet and don't use old seeds leftover from a previous season. The viability of the seeds reduces dramatically after they age even one year.

NAME:	Parsnip, #2
YIELD/FOOT (LB.)	8.00
COST/LB.	$4.46
VALUE	$35.68
INPUT	$0.64
ROI	$35.04
ROI%	5,475%

Cherry

Heirloom

TOMATOES

This garden classic tops many lists of the favorite edible of home gardeners across the country. And for lots of good reasons. The astounding number of tomato varieties offers an incredible range of sizes, flavors, and even appearances. Tomatoes come in rainbow of colors and even patterns, and among the options there is undoubtedly something for everyone.

One of the first choices you'll have to make, though, is whether the variety is determinate or indeterminate. Determinate are bush-type tomatoes with a limited harvest period, while indeterminate are vining plants that can provide a continuous or repeat harvest, making indeterminate the most popular type. If you have trouble remembering the difference between determinate and indeterminate type tomato plants, here is a hint I use. Because the determinate types are bush plants, you know ahead of time how tall they will grow before the growth stops. That's determinate. Vine types of tomato plants will just keep growing and growing till they are killed by the fall frost, and that is indeterminate.

Regardless of variety, look for pest- and disease-resistant varieties. The plants or seeds will be labeled "VFN," indicating resistance to Verticillium wilt (V), Fusarium wilt (F) and nematodes (N). These can all kill tomato plants virtually overnight.

It's always a good idea to plant several different types and varieties, beginning with the mix of available sizes.

Cherry: Although we've used the most common type of miniature as the listing title, this category includes cherry, currant, and grape tomatoes. They are all bite-size packages of flavor great for picking and eating right in the garden and are ideal for a child's garden. Try any variety of black cherry tomatoes for an extraordinary flavor and unusual appearance.

Heirloom: These are varieties that have been passed down through generations (usually 50 years old or more) and have been bred with open pollination between plants for distinctive characteristics. They include some of the most exotic tomatoes with unusual shapes and flavors that make them a favorite in specialty markets and home gardens. Sample any striped variety for an uncommon look in a slicing tomato.

Hybrid: Hybrids are varieties that have been intentionally cross-pollinated to create highly desirable combinations. They are the most common tomatoes. Consider the 'SteakHouse Hybrid' for a super large beefsteak.

Hybrid

Roma

Roma: These thick-walled, fleshy, compact tomatoes were developed in Italy as the base for classic sauces and tomato paste. The Roma is not considered a great eating tomato because they are less juicy than other types, but they are wonderful when cooked. Check out orange varieties for a wonderful addition to homemade salsa.

Although you can grow tomatoes from seed, many gardeners find the process a bit challenging. Seedlings are the more common start, and any purchased seedling should be buried deep—covering about two-thirds of the plant to encourage a strong root system. Just make sure you pinch off any branches and leaves that will be below ground so they do not rot.

Value Added:

- For the healthiest, biggest tomato harvest year to year, alternate crops in any given location. By moving your tomato plants around, you lessen the possibility of losing one or more of your plants to soil-borne diseases. This is true of many vegetables. Crop rotation is very important, and makes records doubly important. Next year, you can look up where everything was so you won't plant the same thing in the same place.

NAME:	Tomato, cherry, #3	Tomato, heirloom, #5	Tomato, hybrid, #10	Tomato, Roma, #19
YIELD/FOOT (LB.)	8.00	8.00	8.00	8.00
COST/LB.	$3.76	$3.45	$2.51	$1.49
VALUE	$30.08	$27.60	$20.08	$11.92
INPUT	$3.95	$3.95	$3.95	$3.95
ROI	$26.13	$23.65	$16.13	$7.97
ROI%	662%	599%	408%	202%

GARLIC

Garlic is one of the most useful vegetables you can grow, included in many kitchen dishes and excellent even alone, roasted, with a little cheese and bread. Choose from the three basic types of garlic:

Soft neck: The most common and the type found in most supermarkets. Smaller, regular heads, classic garlic flavor.

Hard neck: Has a straw-like center stem, off of which the bulbs form. Hard-neck varieties are larger, with a greater range of flavors than soft neck. 'Killarney Red' is a beautiful, striped garlic with a distinctively nutty flavor.

Elephant: Not technically garlic, but is sold and grown as such. Produces a large, more mild-flavored head.

Plant a bulb from a head of garlic, about 2 inches below the surface of the soil, in fall after the first frost. The soil should be nutritious and well-drained. Plant it with the pointed end up. Mulch the site well. Do not plant garlic where any other member of the onion family has recently grown.

In spring, leaves and stalks will grow, until they stop in early summer. When the stalks are brown, carefully dig up the bulbs and store or use. Kept in a cool, dark location with good air circulation, garlic bulbs can last months.

Value Added:

- Put your garlic to work as a pest deterrence for other plants in your garden. Garlic is a common companion plant to tomatoes and roses, and it deters aphids and Japanese beetles.

- Garlic makes wonderful housewarming and dinner party gifts. Leave the long dried stalks intact after harvesting and braid them together.

NAME:	Garlic, #4
YIELD/FOOT (LB.)	6.75
COST/LB.	$3.75
VALUE	$25.31
INPUT	$0.10
ROI	$25.21
ROI%	25,213%

TURNIP

This is another cool-weather crop that is actually two crops in one. The roots are filling vegetables while the greens make highly nutritious and flavorful additions to salads or a side dish braised with pork or ham.

You can plant turnips in spring or fall, but fall is often the better choice. Sudden heat in early summer can cause the greens to go bitter. As summer comes on, the plants will bolt. Turnips love rich, well-drained soil. Plant seeds about two months before the last frost date in spring, and ten weeks before the first frost date in fall. You may be able to grow the root over winter in mild southern regions with no winter freeze.

Turnips are ready for harvest when the tops are about 8 inches tall and the roots are about 3 inches in diameter. You can harvest them young without losing any flavor. If you're using the greens, they are best cooked as soon as they are cut. They will only keep in a refrigerator for two to three days.

Value Added:

- Turnip greens will eventually yellow and die during the season. Removing them as they do will encourage further leaf growth. The same is true of harvesting greens as the plant grows.

- If you love turnip greens, overplant. Crowd the plants together when seeding, and wait for the greens to get just big enough to pick, and then harvest the entire plant to thin out the plot. It's a great way to have abundant greens and plenty of turnips.

NAME:	Turnip, #6
YIELD/FOOT (LB.)	9.00
COST/LB.	$2.55
VALUE	$22.95
INPUT	$0.09
ROI	$22.86
ROI%	25,400%

LEEK

Leeks are a misunderstood garden gem. Offering a more elegant, understated flavor than yellow or white onions, leeks are every bit as easy to grow if you understand just a little bit of what this plant needs to thrive.

Choose the best leek for your location. Colder, northern regions are generally better suited to the less-hardy "short season" varieties, planted in spring and harvested in late summer or fall. Long-season varieties can take almost four months to mature and are hardy enough to grow into winter in warmer southern zones.

No matter where or when you're planting your leeks, you'll want to create a loamy, nitrogen-rich bed that drains well but retains moisture. Leeks like near-constant moisture.

As the plants mature, mound soil up to the bottom of the greens. This ensures that the more flavorful white portion remains pure white and tasty.

You can harvest leeks young to use as you would scallions, but you get the best flavor from mature leeks that are 1 inch or more in diameter. Loosen the soil before pulling them up to protect against breakage or damage.

Value Added:

- A little bit of soil in the rings of a leek can ruin a dish. Although it's always wise to clean leeks thoroughly before cooking with them, you can protect against soil infiltrating between layers by slipping a cardboard toilet paper tube down over the seedling's green stalks. The tube will eventually rot away, but will prevent any soil you mound from making its way down into the growing vegetable.

- If you're growing a Square Foot Garden, try the high-yield method of using the top hat, which is a no-work, no-mounding method that we use for all root crops such as potatoes, leeks, and scallions that will produce almost twice the harvest of that desirable white stem.

NAME:	Leek, #7		
YIELD/FOOT (LB.)	9.00		
COST/LB.	$2.11		
VALUE	$18.99		
INPUT	$0.27		
ROI	$18.72		
ROI%	6,933%		

SQUASH, WINTER

The sprawling vines of winter squash can be intimidating to some gardeners who don't want their yard or garden taken over by one crop. But you can keep squash plants in check and healthier by growing the crop up a trellis or other vertical support.

This is an unusual vegetable, picked only at the end of fall, when the skin has hardened and the vines die. Because of the thick skin on a mature squash, these beauties keep for a good long time—deep into winter—without losing a bit of their pleasingly rich and sweet flavor.

Plant at least two presoaked seeds per hole and snip off the smallest seedling if both seeds sprout. It pays to keep the soil moist during the season, and weed as necessary, although the leafy vines often shade out most weed growth.

Harvest the squash after the first light frost kills the vines and leaves, but before a hard freeze. Cut the stem from the vine with pruners, leaving at least 1 inch of stem. Then wipe clean and cure the squash in a sun-drenched spot that warms to around 70 degrees Fahrenheit during the day, protecting it at night. Leave it out for two weeks to fully cure.

NAME:	Squash, Winter, #8				
YIELD/FOOT (LB.)	15.00				
COST/LB.	$1.23				
VALUE	$18.45				
INPUT	$0.30				
ROI	$18.15				
ROI%	6,050%				

Value Added:

- Winter squash grows both male and female flowers that must cross-pollinate for the fruits to grow. However, harvest one or two of the male blossoms (the first ones that bloom on the plant) as a lovely decorative edible to add to salads.

SPINACH

Nutritious and flavorful, spinach is a favorite leafy green of gardeners everywhere for its versatility in the kitchen. However, many home gardeners find it a challenge to grow because it simply won't tolerate heat. The trick is to plant as early as possible for a spring crop.

The plants will grow in partial shade, making it a little easier to keep them cool. Spinach is usually planted from seed because it doesn't transplant well. Plant as early as feasible in spring, drop seeds into a ½-inch deep hole and cover with a plastic cold frame or cover. Make sure the soil is rich and nutritious and keep the soil constantly moist during the growing season.

You can help your spinach plants endure warming weather by heavily mulching around the plants. You don't have to worry about diseases with spinach, but do keep an eye out for aphids and leaf miners.

Harvest the outer leaves as soon as the plant is bushy. You can continue to harvest whatever you need as the spinach grows, but when the weather heats up and you suspect the plant will bolt, pull the entire plant and use the remaining leaves for a side dish or salad.

Value Added:

- If you live in a temperate zone or region, maximize your garden value by growing the spinach beyond fall and into winter. As long as the plant doesn't freeze, there's a good chance it will produce all through winter.

- Next to water, spinach loves nitrogen. Side-dress the plants with an organic nitrogen fertilizer for bigger leaves and bushier plants.

NAME:	Spinach, #9
YIELD/FOOT (LB.)	6.75
COST/LB.	$2.89
VALUE	$19.51
INPUT	$2.97
ROI	$16.54
ROI%	557%

MUSTARD GREENS

Combining the allure of lettuce and the complex flavor of sturdier greens such as collards and kale, mustard greens are a wonderful addition to a salad-producing vegetable garden. The flavor is spicier and more peppery than other greens, making mustard greens excellent for salads or sandwiches. These cool-season greens are also relatively fast growing and highly nutritious.

Although seed companies recommend planting many seeds in one hole, thin your plants, or seedlings before planting, to ensure the bushiest growth possible. As soon as the seedlings establish and become robust, a hit of fertilizer will ensure bushy, thick, and quick leaf growth.

The plants are not overly susceptible to insects or disease, but do keep an eye out for cabbage loopers and cabbageworms.

Gardeners harvest mustard greens in one of two ways: taking just the outside leaves, or cutting down the entire plant, leaving a couple of inches at the base to regrow. Choose depending the quantity of greens you'll be able to use at one time. In any case, you can harvest the first leaves about a month after planting when they are about 6 inches long.

As with other cool-weather greens, a light fall frost will add sweetness to mustard greens. In fact, you may be able to grow the greens deep into winter in southern zones.

NAME:	Mustard greens, #11
YIELD/FOOT (LB.)	8.00
COST/LB.	$2.01
VALUE	$16.08
INPUT	$2.18
ROI	$13.90
ROI%	638%

Value Added:
- For optimum harvest, avoid stressing your mustard green plants. These are sensitive garden greens that don't like drought or heat. Keep the soil moist and ensure the plants don't overheat.

Red

ONION (YELLOW, WHITE, RED)

Onions are some of the most practical crops you can grow, not only because they have so many uses in the kitchen, but also because they can keep for months if properly stored. There are subtle differences in cultivation between the three basic types of onions, even though any onion is very easy to grow. Within these three, you'll find an amazing number of varieties from which to choose—all offering their own unique flavors. Red, white, or yellow hybrids will last months once harvested and dried, but certain types of onions need to be used fairly soon after harvesting.

Onions can be planted from seeds, seedlings, or "sets"—small bulbs. If your cool-weather growing season is short, it's best to plant sets. Otherwise, you can quite easily grow from seeds.

Red onions are the sweetest type of onion and are wonderful pickled. Red are the best choice among onions to grow from a set. To plant a set, dig the hole about 2 inches deep and drop the set in the hole root-end down. (The root end is the brown, flat side.) Choose 'Red Creole' for a spicier flavor, or grow a red cipollini for a tiny, surpassingly sweet red onion.

If you cook for a large family, you might want to select a bigger variety of yellow onion, such as 'Big Daddy'. The traditional 'Walla, Walla, Sweet' has a signature flavor and is incredibly versatile. The white 'Exhibition' is a sweet version of the white's usually mild flavor.

Keep an eye out for thrips and treat them with insecticidal soap. You may occasionally experience onion maggots. If so, cover unaffected plants completely with netting, mounding soil around the base of the netting to create an enclosed net tent.

Onions generally don't need any fertilizer help, and avoid adding nitrogen to your soil, which can cause greater top growth and a smaller onion bulb. The plants will only need a weekly watering, and you should stop watering once the tops start to fall over and brown.

All bulb onions are harvested the same way. As the stalks turn yellow, you may want to force them over with a rake, so that the plant's energy is refocused to the bulb. Loosen

Yellow

White

the soil around the onion and pull it up. Lay the harvest on a window screen or chicken wire for several days, until the paper covering and top dry out. Onions with green or thick tops should be used within one or two days.

Value Added:

- Be aware that if you choose to plant your onions from sets, the plant will be more prone to bolting than it would otherwise be. That is why sets are better in regions with cooler summers. If you decide to plant sets, pick out ½-inch bulbs, which are less likely to bolt.

- Plant radish seeds along with your onions for a trap crop that will draw root maggots away from the onions.

NAME:	Onion, yellow, #12	Onion, white, #18	Onion, red, #20
YIELD/FOOT (LB.)	16.00	12.00	8.00
COST/LB.	$0.83	$0.87	$1.13
VALUE	$13.28	$10.44	$9.04
INPUT	$1.28	$1.28	$1.33
ROI	$12.00	$9.16	$7.71
ROI%	938%	716%	580%

PUMPKIN

Pumpkins are definitely in the running for the title of most purely fun crop you can grow. This fall crop needs the right site, with nutritious soil, lots of sun, and a steady supply of water right through harvest.

Choose your variety carefully, because they range through different weight classes from "mini" or "small" (less than 5 pounds), through medium (up to about 15 pounds), and on to large (up to 25 pounds). There are "jumbo" varieties that can grow up to 100 pounds, although these are mostly fascination crops.

All can be used for decorative or culinary purposes, but it's wise to eat the pumpkins you grow because they are chock full of nutrients and fiber. Not to mention the unique and subtly sweet flavor is a memorable flavor to add to any meal.

Be prepared to handle the long-growing vines, and water with drip irrigation to avoid the hassle of hand watering (don't ever let water sit on the leaves or you risk disease). You can also grow the vines up a trellis, as long as you provide proper support for the mature fruits.

You'll know your pumpkins are ready for harvest when the vines and leaves yellow and begin to die.

Value Added:

- Control vine flowers to determine size and number of pumpkins. Pinch main vine tips when the vines are 2 feet long and you'll get more pumpkins in a more compact plant. Increase your yield another way by pinching off all female flowers for the first three weeks. However, when you increase production, you decrease the size of the pumpkins. For fewer, larger pumpkins, pinch off all remaining flowers after three or four fruits have formed.

NAME:	Pumpkin, #13
YIELD/FOOT (LB.)	24.00
COST/LB.	$0.50
VALUE	$12.00
INPUT	$0.24
ROI	$11.76
ROI%	4,900%

LETTUCE

Decide to grow lettuce in your garden and you'll have plenty of options from which to choose. Frankly, the best strategy may involve planting several different types for a range of flavors and textures in your salad bowl. In any case, lettuces are cool-weather crops ideal for early spring and fall plantings.

All lettuces prefer strong direct sun, but will grow in partly shady conditions (and a little shade may slow down the process of bolting in hot weather). Most will adapt to spacing, so although you should plant to the maximum listed spacing if you have plenty of room in your garden, you can certainly crowd more plants in if you're dealing with a tight fit in your particular backyard (or containers).

NAME:	Lettuce, Mesclun, #14	Lettuce, Romaine, #17	Lettuce, Green/Red, #22	Lettuce, Butter, #25
YIELD/FOOT (LB.)	2.00	9.00	6.75	4.50
COST/LB.	$5.99	$1.22	$1.17	$1.37
VALUE	$11.98	$10.98	$7.90	$6.17
INPUT	$0.36	$0.36	$0.36	$0.36
ROI	$11.62	$10.62	$7.54	$5.81
ROI%	3,228%	2,950%	2,094%	1,613%

These are thirsty plants, so make sure they get abundant water. But take care that no water sits on the leaves, because standing water can spread fungal diseases. These plants also grow from shallow roots, so their beds need to be weed free because they can't compete with the deeper roots of weeds.

Aphids, slugs, and snails are the most common pests that attack lettuces, but all three are easy to deal with and eradicate. Either handpick, use insecticidal soap, and/or a shallow saucer of stale beer.

Harvesting techniques should be determined by how much lettuce your family will eat at one time, and your own preferences. You'll get the most out of any lettuce plants by harvesting the outer leaves as they mature. But that may make it difficult to throw together a large salad for the whole family. You can also wait until the entire plant is mature and harvest the entire head or all the leaves at once. You'll get the biggest harvest if you plant a lot of lettuces and start harvesting leaves as soon as they are half grown. They will still taste delicious, and the strategy will spare you the inconvenience of harvesting all the mature plants at once.

In any case, harvest the entire plant if it is threatening to bolt or daytime temperatures are rising significantly. Once a lettuce plant begins the process of bolting— sending up flower stalks that in turn become seedheads—the entire plant will become displeasingly bitter.

Value Added:

- If time is an issue or you just don't want to start plants indoors, you can buy seedlings rather than sowing directly into your garden. Keep in mind, though, that transplants are more susceptible to early bolting.

- Get the most out of your salad greens by picking the leaves early in the morning, rinsing them in a colander and letting them air dry. They'll be ready and waiting for the salad as soon as you start making dinner.

ARUGULA

Arugula is a wonderful salad green with a lot of potential uses in the kitchens. In the garden, its value is most affected by ability to grow fast with little effort on the gardener's part. It's considered a cool-season annual, but if your location has mild summers or you can keep it in a cool, partly shaded area, you may be able to grow this green right through summer. Usually though, you'll get two to three harvests in spring and fall.

'Bellezia' has finer leaves, making it look like wild arugula and adding visual interest to any salad bowl. 'Selvatica Organic' is a little more heat tolerant than normal, and intensely flavorful.

If you cut the outer leaves, you may be able to get a repeat harvest from the same plant. In most cases, though, the greens will be ready to harvest two to three weeks after planting, and you can replant right after harvesting (something assumed in the calculations for this crop). Ensure against excess heat, which can result in a more bitter green. As with most salad greens, good drainage is a must, and arugula grows just as well in the ground, in raised beds, and in containers.

NAME:	Arugula, #15
YIELD/FOOT (LB.)	2.00
COST/LB.	$8.00
VALUE	$16.00
INPUT	$4.99
ROI	$11.01
ROI%	221%

Value Added:

- If you value beauty in your garden, allow your arugula to bolt, and you'll find it grows delightful white flowers. The blooms are themselves edible, and wonderful additions to salads (for more edible flowers, see the box on page 116). Provide a mini-greenhouse over the crop and you may optimize value by having arugula into winter.

CUCUMBER

Cucumbers are some of the most refreshing vegetables to come from the garden. They also offer the opportunity to experiment with unusual varieties—including long and short, ball and lemon, and English hothouse cucumbers with their distinctively light and floral flavor.

You'll have to decide between bush and vine varieties. Bush cucumbers produce less of a harvest but are easier to manage in the garden. Vine cucumber plants sprawl over a large area. You can, however, grow these on trellises to better control and confine the growth and keep the plants healthier.

The vegetable itself is largely water, which means cucumber plants are thirsty garden plantings. Water at least twice weekly and make sure the plant never shows sign of wilting.

Harvesting cucumbers correctly is crucial to maintaining plant health and productivity. It's better to harvest and compost cucumbers you aren't ready to eat than it is to leave them on the vine. It's also okay to pick cucumbers slightly smaller than normal—they'll be just as delicious. In either case, cut the stem that connects the cucumber to the main vine. Do not pull the fruit or you risk damaging the plant.

Value Added:

- Never let any of the cucumbers on your plant mature to the point of yellowing and softening. If this happens, it slows down production on the whole plant, costing you overall yield.

- Get the most out of cucumbers fresh from your garden by slicing them with the peel left on. The peel holds much of the vegetable's nutrients.

NAME:	Cucumber, #16
YIELD/FOOT (LB.)	9.00
COST/LB.	$1.23
VALUE	$11.07
INPUT	$0.36
ROI	$10.71
ROI%	2,975%

WATERMELON

You can buy seedless and seeded varieties of watermelon and pick from an amazing diversity of sizes, shapes, and appearances—from tiny two-person fruits to jumbo party pleasers.

Get your watermelons off to a good start by amending the soil to create a rich foundation. Although watermelons grow reliably from seed, the maturation period is so long—and the seed needs warm soil to germinate (the soil needs to be above 70 degrees Fahrenheit for the seeds to germinate)—that anyone gardening in cooler, northern regions will need to either start seeds indoors or plant seedlings once the soil warms.

Be aware that this is a large, sprawling vine plant that takes up space and is unruly. Plan for the growth. You can grow many smaller varieties on a well-supported, reinforced trellis. You must support each melon. Panty hose is ideal to slip over the melon and then tie to the trellis framework.

The plants can be damaged by cucumber beetles and vine borers. Use a floating row cover for young plants, and remove it when male and female flowers appear.

Determining when watermelon is ripe is as much art as science. On some varieties, the vine tendril closest to the fruit will wither and die, but that isn't universal. A more reliable indicator—if you haven't been turning the fruit—is to check the bottom spot where the melon as been sitting. When ripe, that spot will turn from white to a deep yellow.

NAME:	Watermelon, #21
YIELD/FOOT (LB.)	15.00
COST/LB.	$0.58
VALUE	$8.70
INPUT	$0.99
ROI	$7.71
ROI%	779%

Value Added:
- Getting the sweetest melons possible is the way to eke out the best value from your plants. When the vines begin to sprawl, dissolve 1 tablespoon borax into 1 gallon water and spray the leaves and base of the plant.

STRAWBERRY

It's the rare gardener who wouldn't enjoy a crop of this sweet, delicious fruit. But if you're adding strawberries to your outdoor grocery store, you'll need to decide which of the three you want to plant.

June-bearing: Produces one large crop in early, mid-, or late summer, depending on the variety. June-bearing are a good choice if you're making jams or freezing the harvest.

Everbearing: Produces a large crop during longer days full of sunlight. That means a big crop at the start of summer, some throughout, and a smaller crop in early fall.

Day-neutral: Provides a continuous harvest peaking once each summer month. Production stops when temperatures run higher than 80 degrees Fahrenheit and the berries are a bit smaller than other types.

The easiest way to plant strawberries is from starts (plants from seeds can take up to three years to bear fruit), and you can mix types in the same bed for a more or less continuous harvest. Cut runners regularly to keep the plant's energy directed to growing fruit. Keep the soil moist and mulch heavily to ensure the roots are kept cool.

Harvest the fruit by cutting the connecting stem when the berry is large and fully red. If you keep on eye on your plants and water at soil level, you'll rarely have to deal with diseases. However, keep an eye out for slugs.

Value Added:

- Much as you might love birds and wildlife in your garden, protect the value of your strawberry harvest by covering plants with bird netting. These sweet fruits are just too tempting to winged garden visitors.

NAME:	Strawberry, #23
YIELD/FOOT (LB.)	3.00
COST/LB.	$3.43
VALUE	$10.29
INPUT	$2.84
ROI	$7.45
ROI%	262%

ZUCCHINI (SUMMER SQUASH)

Zucchini is famous as one of the most prolific edible plants you can grow in your garden. That big yield doesn't come in a tidy package, though. Zucchini vines are vigorous and rambling, and tend to take up a lot of space in the garden. You can keep them a little more in control by growing zucchini up a trellis or other support.

Either way, like other squashes, zucchini loves water. Start with nutritious, compost-amended soil and keep the soil moist all through the season. Water at the base of the plants and try to avoid getting the leaves wet, which can lead to disease.

The plant does well from seeds if they are planted about a week after the last frost, when the temperature outside is above 60 degrees Fahrenheit.

If the plants grow flowers but don't fruit, it may be that insects are not transferring pollen from the male to the female flowers. You can do this manually with a cotton swab. Swab a bit of pollen from inside the male, and then rub the pollen on the stigma in the center of the female flowers.

Err on the side of an early harvest, because zucchini are more flavorful and tender while they're young. Start removing individual fruits as soon as they are 4 inches long.

NAME:	Zucchini, #24		
YIELD/FOOT (LB.)	4.50		
COST/LB.	$1.55		
VALUE	$6.98		
INPUT	$0.18		
ROI	$6.80		
ROI%	3,775%		

Value Added:

- Female squash blossoms are a delicacy and a way to get more out of each zucchini. Harvest a few while they're young (you'll be sacrificing a few zucchini) and then batter them and deep fry for a wonderful treat.

RADICCHIO

This unique and beautiful leafy vegetable is cultivated much like cabbage. It's a cool-weather crop that can actually be grown as a perennial in some locations if proper care is taken to prevent freezing. No matter when you grow it, it is a pleasantly bitter addition to salads.

Plant in spring as early as the soil is workable. For fall harvest, plant mid-to late summer unless you experience mild winters, in which case early fall is fine. Provide shade against strong summer sun. Water consistently regardless of season, because dry spells can make the leaves unpleasantly bitter. Water even more heavily just as the heads are maturing.

You can harvest the leaves any time during the season, for accents with other greens. Cut off the entire head at soil level when it is as firm as iceberg lettuce. Don't let the head get too mature or the leaves will become too bitter.

Radicchio can bolt (although you'll find many "bolt-resistant" varieties on the market), which will be evident when a hard core starts to form in the head. That will be followed by a flower stem growing up. Radicchio is less likely to bolt in the fall, and a light frost will add sweetness to the leaves.

Value Added:

- Coax your radicchio into returning as a perennial by cutting the stem slightly higher than soil level, then providing protection against freezing weather. Some gardeners use an overturned plant pot, or you can mulch with several inches of straw or similar mulch.

NAME:	Radicchio, #26
YIELD/FOOT (LB.)	1.50
COST/LB.	$5.19
VALUE	$7.79
INPUT	$2.00
ROI	$5.79
ROI%	289%

KOHLRABI

Kohlrabi is an unusual relative to cabbage, with similarities to turnips and other roots. Although home gardeners may not be well-acquainted with the vegetable, there's good reason to include it in a backyard garden. Kohlrabi provides both an edible tuber and edible leaves—both with a pleasant, mild, and sweet flavor. It also offers the same high level of nutrition present in cabbage and related leafy greens—all in a package that matures much quicker than its relatives. Plant 'Azur Star' for a stunning purple root and stems that will liven up any dinner table.

This is a cool-weather crop that doesn't do well in heat. It's regularly grown in fall and spring, and needs only about two months from sowing to harvesting. Like similar crops, a light frost will improve the flavor of both the leaves and the bulb.

Kohlrabi is generally less susceptible to insect attack and is resistant to most diseases that affect leafy greens.

Harvest the entire bulb and leaves at the same time. It's better to err on the side of immaturity when it comes to kohlrabi, because young bulbs will be a bit more tender and flavorful. The greens should be used immediately, but the bulb, trimmed of stems and leaves, can be wrapped in plastic and stored in the refrigerator for more than a month.

Value Added:
- Like many members of the cabbage family, kohlrabi is a thirsty plant. Ensure the tastiest, healthiest bulb by supplying 1 to 2 inches of water per week continuously throughout the growing season.

NAME:	Kohlrabi, #27
YIELD/FOOT (LB.)	4.00
COST/LB.	$1.50
VALUE	$6.00
INPUT	$0.60
ROI	$5.40
ROI%	900%

FENNEL (BULB)

Fennel has a long and storied history as a sturdy Mediterranean vegetable. Although it will grow in many zones, it will survive as a perennial only in the warmest parts of the country, usually Zones 9 and 10. In either case, the vegetable is a worthy addition to your garden.

Ancient Romans revered the plant for its curative properties, as an aid to digestion, and a weight-control food. It is valued in modern times for the delicate licorice flavor. To get the most out of the plant, use the bulb as a vegetable, the foliage as a herb and garnish, and the dried seed as spice.

Sow seed after the last frost in spring. Fennel can tolerate drought conditions, but does need rich, well-drained soil. Cut the fronds as needed, once they are 8 inches long (as long as at least half the foliage is left, the bulb will continue to develop). Harvest the bulb after three months, as soon as it is about 3 inches across. Dig down and slice under the bulb to separate it from the long taproot.

Value Added:

- Along with its culinary uses, you can also plant fennel as a garden helper. It's pretty enough for ornamental beds and attracts beneficial insects to the garden.

- Get even more out of fennel flowers by drying them and then placing them in a jar filled with olive oil. Let the jar sit in a cool, dark place for a week and you'll have a wonderful flavored oil for use on pork or vegetables you're about to grill.

NAME:	Fennel #28
YIELD/FOOT (LB.)	1.50
COST/LB.	$3.26
VALUE	$4.89
INPUT	$0.15
ROI	$4.74
ROI%	3,160%

EGGPLANT

Eggplants are some of the most beautiful vegetables you can grow in your garden. As lovely as the traditional purple, teardrop-shaped varieties look, you can also opt for ball-shaped, striped, and even white versions like 'Crescent Moon' for a totally unexpected look.

The two things any eggplants love when growing are heat and water. This is a full-sun plant. Provide a consistent supply of water, especially as the fruits mature.

You may need to stake plants when the eggplant get close to maturity, because the weight of the fruit can pull the plant over.

Harvesting eggplants is a bit of an art. Use the thumbprint test. If the fruit is unripe, you won't be able to press your thumb into the surface of the fruit. If it's ripe, your thumb should leave a slight indentation that will quickly disappear. If you can make an indentation in the surface that stays that way, the fruit is overripe—pick any others on the plant more quickly.

The fruit should be large, plump, and glossy. It's better to harvest slightly early rather than late, because overly mature eggplants will have large, hard, and bitter seeds making the vegetable less than palatable.

Value Added:

- If you're buying starter plants from a nursery, select ones with thick stems and no flowers. They will give your eggplants the best possible start and chance for success.

- Help your eggplants grow strong by keeping the soil around the plants free of any weeds. Weeds will steal essential nutrients from the vegetable plants.

NAME:	Eggplant, #29
YIELD/FOOT (LB.)	6.00
COST/LB.	$1.40
VALUE	$8.40
INPUT	$3.95
ROI	$4.45
ROI%	113%

CANTALOUPE (MUSKMELON)

This sweet fruit likes it hot. Or, more specifically, the leaves like it hot. The leaves are crucial for the fruit development and they are especially key to the sugar content. That means not only giving the leaves the benefit of a hot growing season, but also ample water and keeping them free of disease.

If your local climate does not feature a very hot summer, you can help the vines grow by laying black sheeting under the plant, or behind it if you're growing vertically. No matter how you grow the plant, ensure that it receives ample water, but do not let water sit on the leaves because that can lead to disease.

It is fairly obvious when the fruit is ripe; the surface pattern becomes pronounced and the yellow color deepens. The stem may also show a crack. Hold the stem in one hand and the fruit in the other. The melon should twist off with virtually no resistance. If it doesn't, the fruit isn't fully ripe.

Eat cantaloupe within two days or refrigerate for up to five days. You can also cut up the flesh and freeze it for a fantastic smoothie additive.

Value Added:

- Make the most of available space and ensure the health of your cantaloupe plants by growing them vertically. As long as you provide stable support, the melons will mature just as they would on the ground, but without the risk of disease and rot.

- The most valuable cantaloupe is the sweetest. To ensure the highest sugar content in your cantaloupes, taper off watering when the fruit is almost completely ripe.

NAME:	Cantaloupe, #30
YIELD/FOOT (LB.)	8.00
COST/LB.	$0.62
VALUE	$4.96
INPUT	$1.00
ROI	$3.96
ROI%	396%

Heirloom

CARROT

Hybrid

Carrots are some of the simplest and most satisfying vegetables to grow. Between hybrids and heirlooms, you can find varieties in every color of the rainbow and shapes ranging from long and pencil-thin to globe.

All carrots need consistently moist soil—never let the soil completely dry out until the carrots are nearly mature. Too much watering is just as bad; it can cause the carrots to split.

Carrots do best in loose, sandy soil that allows for straight growth. If your soil is less than ideal, consider growing a "ball" variety.

It's better to harvest carrots early, rather than late, and "baby" carrots are excellent in any meal. The younger the carrot, the sweeter and more tender it will be.

Extra carrots can be pickled and put up. But they can also be stored over winter in a cool, dark area such as a basement, root cellar, or even a shed. Twist off the carrot tops to prevent moisture loss, then store between layers of sand, with no carrots touching. Top with a thick layer of straw for fresh carrots throughout the winter.

Value Added:

- To get the most nutrition out of your carrots, scrub them clean but don't peel them. Most of the vitamins in this vegetable reside close to the surface and peeling a carrot removes nutrients.

NAME:	Carrot, Heirloom, #31	Carrot, Hybrid, #39
YIELD/FOOT (LB.)	2.25	2.25
COST/LB.	$1.85	$0.87
VALUE	$3.70	$1.96
INPUT	$0.25	$0.23
ROI	$3.45	$1.73
ROI%	1,380%	751%

RADISH, DAIKON

Although closely related the common spring radishes found in American supermarkets, the Daikon is one of a smaller number of winter radishes, which require a much longer growing period (most varieties need about 70 days to mature) and a bit more care. But make no mistake, these reward the astute gardener with superior longevity, a more complex flavor, and a longer life in the refrigerator.

The white Daikon is only the most common color. You can find purple, red, and green as well. Although these radishes need the moist soil that spring radishes crave, avoid overwatering them, which can lead to rot.

You may want to harvest your Daikon crop early, because fully mature Daikon radishes are somewhat tougher than other radishes. But they are also very adaptable. In Asia, these radishes aren't just eaten raw; they find their way into soups, stews, stir-fries, and other cooked dishes.

Value Added:

- Daikon radishes have value in the garden even if you don't want to use them in the kitchen or prefer a more conventional radish flavor. They can be planted as a sacrificial trap crop to lure flea beetles and other pests from eating cabbage and lettuces.

- Daikons can actually be left in the soil over mild winters and harvested in early spring. However, these radishes will be larger than normal, with a diminished flavor and woody texture.

- Daikon leaves are an effective "green manure." Cut them off as you harvest the radishes and then plow them under to improve the soil for the crop to follow.

NAME:	Radish, #32
YIELD/FOOT (LB.)	2.00
COST/LB.	$1.86
VALUE	$3.72
INPUT	$0.36
ROI	$3.36
ROI%	933%

COLLARD GREENS

Although known as a Southern specialty, collard greens are actually a cool-weather crop that is slightly more heat resistant than relatives cabbage, broccoli, and kale. Plant in spring or fall, although fall plantings are often the better choice because collard greens aren't bothered by early frosts.

The trick to getting a good crop from your collard green plants is spurring quick initial growth. Plant the seeds in very nutritious soil with a pH between 6.0 and 7.5. Ensure a continuous supply of water that keeps the soil slightly moist, and mulch heavily to reduce moisture loss.

Collard greens fall prey to the same insects and diseases that attack cabbage plants, so a floating row cover is a good idea for young plants.

You can harvest individual leaves as needed (always take lower leaves first, to ensure tenderness), or cut down the entire head all at once. In parts of the country with mild winters, you may be able to harvest the plant throughout winter. Leaves should keep in a vegetable crisper for up to a week.

NAME:	Collard Greens, #33
YIELD/FOOT (LB.)	3.48
COST/LB.	$0.96
VALUE	$3.34
INPUT	$0.15
ROI	$3.19
ROI%	2,127%

Value Added:

- Want a little better flavor for your collard green investment? This cold-loving vegetable is sweeter after a light frost.

- You get the most from your collard greens by braising or adding to soups and stews. Although the cooked greens make a wonderful side dish with bits of ham or bacon, fresh collard greens are an acquired taste. Use raw in a green smoothie with sweet fruit to offset the flavor—it's a super-nutritious, one-glass meal.

CORN

Corn is one of the all-time favorite summer vegetables, prized for the deliciously sweet kernels captured in an eat-with-your-hands package. Because it is so popular, you'll find a head-spinning diversity of varieties (even including purple varieties such as 'Suntava'). But for the sweetest corn, turn to white rather than pure yellow, and bi-color as the sweetest of all.

The seeds are easy to plant and grow, but pests are a common problem when it comes to growing corn. Not only are ear worms and corn borers regular uninvited guests to the vegetable, many types of wildlife find maturing ears of corn a delicacy like no other. That's why corn should be grown in an area offering at least some protection from predators such as crows, raccoons, and deer.

You'll know your corn has made it safely to maturity when the silk begins to turn brown and the ear feels firm and bumpy. Before picking, peel down a small strip of husk to check that the kernels are plump. Pierce one and it should leak milky fluid—if the liquid is clear, the ear is not ready for harvesting. To remove the ear without damaging the stalk, hold the stalk firm with one hand and twist off the ear with the other.

Value Added:

- Ensure your efforts to grow seedlings are rewarded with mature, harvestable crops by protecting young corn plants. A chicken-wire cage over corn seedlings can stop birds and other wildlife from eating your crop before you get a chance to.

NAME:	Corn, #34
YIELD/FOOT (LB.)	4.50
COST/LB.	$0.66
VALUE	$2.97
INPUT	$0.10
ROI	$2.87
ROI%	2,870%

Savoy

CABBAGE

Cabbage is a hardy, cool-weather crop that provides a bounty of nutrients in a versatile leafy vegetable. All types of cabbage are amazingly adaptable in the kitchen. The leafy vegetable comes in a variety of intriguing and appealing forms that look great on the plate. All cabbages contain valuable vitamins as well as cancer-preventing compounds. (See page 98 for more cancer-fighters from the garden.)

NAME:	Cabbage, Savoy, #35	Cabbage, Napa, #37	Cabbage, Red, #46	Cabbage, Green, #48
YIELD/FOOT (LB.)	2.25	2.25	1.75	2.00
COST/LB.	$1.49	$1.19	$0.59	$0.50
VALUE	$3.35	$2.68	$1.03	$1.00
INPUT	$0.50	$0.50	$0.40	$0.40
ROI	$2.85	$2.18	$0.63	$0.60
ROI%	571%	436%	158%	150%

Green

Savoy: The crispy white heart and delicate crinkled leaves make this a cross between a cabbage and Romaine lettuce. Consider 'Deadon' for a savoy with stunning frilled, magenta leaves.

Napa: Also known as Chinese Cabbage, it straddles the crisp lightness of lettuce and the earthy, full-flavored nature of a cabbage.

Red: Adds a splash of vibrant color to soups, salads, and other dishes and is especially high in vitamins C and A. Look for an early variety such as 'Red Express'.

Green: A famously sturdy green that is the heart of traditional coleslaw, and can also be used to create filling and nutritious soups. 'Flat Dutch' is an early variety with bright yellow-green leaves that are scintillating in the garden.

The trick to harvesting all but Napa cabbage is to allow the head to get large and firm, but not so firm that it splits due to heat or moisture. When it's ready to be harvested, use a sharp knife to cut the head of cabbage at its base.

Because cabbage grows only in shorter cool seasons, it is rarely planted directly as seeds in the garden. Most likely, you'll plant seedlings, which are widely available at nurseries and home centers early in the season and in fall. The calculations here are based on store-bought transplants, although you can start seeds indoors and increase your return on investment.

Value Added:

- Cut your cabbage head carefully when harvesting, to preserve as many leaves as possible, and the plant may grow several smaller heads as a second harvest.

- Play it safe and protect your investment with row covers or plant netting so that cabbage flies can't land on the young plants and lay eggs. Check your maturing heads regularly for any caterpillars or worms and handpick as necessary.

- If the cool seasons are short where you live, grow "early" varieties or the quicker-maturing Napa cabbage to ensure your time, effort, and garden space pay off.

BROCCOLI

Broccoli is another cool-season crop full of nutrients and available in a number of interesting varieties. You can enjoy the fascinating glow-in-the dark lime green and conical Romanesco looking a little like something from outer space, or the deep grape tones of purple sprouting broccoli. Or opt for a tried-and-true standard like 'De Cicco'.

In any case, broccoli is a moisture-loving plant (never let the soil entirely dry out) that should be watered at soil level to avoid getting the developing heads wet.

Harvest broccoli heads when they appear full and tight. Do not let the buds open or you'll wind up with a bitter, inedible vegetable. Cut the stem at an angle to prevent collected water from causing rot.

Some gardeners make the mistake of thinking the plant is done when the main head is harvested and removing the plant. If you harvest carefully to preserve as many leaves as possible, stems and small heads will grow that can produce a second harvest.

Value Added:

- Beets, onions, garlic, and cauliflower are all natural companions to broccoli. Plant these crops together to ensure the largest yield and protect against losing harvest to disease.

- Cover young broccoli plants with a floating row cover or plant netting to protect your investment against highly destructive cabbage worms.

- Grow several varieties to stretch out the season and ensure against weather that could stunt one variety or another.

- Ensure that your broccoli grows as big as possible by mulching heavily around the plants. Remove competitive weeds as soon as you detect them, and your broccoli will be happy and productive.

NAME:	Broccoli, #36
YIELD/FOOT (LB.)	3.00
COST/LB.	$1.42
VALUE	$4.26
INPUT	$1.50
ROI	$2.76
ROI%	184%

Snow

PEA

The fresh flavor of sugar snap and snow peas screams garden goodness. These cool-weather crops are wonderfully low maintenance.

Plant your snap peas as early in spring as possible. Seedlings don't transplant well, so start from seed. Plant the seeds 1 inch deep, five weeks before the last frost, and provide a cold frame or solar tunnel as needed. As the plants grow, don't let the soil dry out. In fact, water daily if need be when the pods are growing and the weather is heating up. Snow peas can be started even earlier.

Both snap and snow peas should be trained up trellises for maximum production. This is true even for "bush" varieties and those listed as "self trellising."

Harvest the individual pods at any time, because they are delicious even when young. Carefully cut each pod off its stem. Don't let any pods mature to the point where they begin to brown, or plant production will taper off.

These vegetables are best used as soon as after harvesting as possible. If you can't use them right away, store them in the refrigerator, washing them right before use. Keep in mind they are absolutely delicious fresh and raw.

Sugar snap

Value Added:

- To give your pea seeds an added boost and ensure the ultimate harvest, mix presoaked seeds with legume inoculant power.

NAME:	Sugar Snap, #38	Snow, #41
YIELD/FOOT (LB.)	0.50	0.40
COST/LB.	$4.87	$4.15
VALUE	$2.44	$1.66
INPUT	$0.64	$0.64
ROI	$1.80	$1.02
ROI%	280%	159%

KALE

Kale is a cool-weather crop similar to cabbage. This vegetable is hardy and easy to grow, and is considered by nutritionists and medical professionals to be a "superfood" because it is full of so many nutrients in such large amounts.

The vegetable's flavor will be sweeter when grown into cold weather, making it ideal as a fall planting. Even in regions that experience very cold winters, kale can be grown under a cold frame. It will grow in warm weather, but the leaves turn bitter in temperatures above 80 degrees Fahrenheit. The seeds prefer cooler soil in which to germinate.

Producing plentiful nutrients requires nutritious soil; amend with plenty of compost and organic fertilizer prior to planting. It's also wise to mulch the plants liberally and keep the leaves from getting wet.

Harvest the oldest leaves from the bottom of the plant, and compost any leaves that are yellowed, insect-eaten, or too old. You can harvest the entire head at the end of the season, and the kale will keep for up to a week in a plastic bag In the refrigerator.

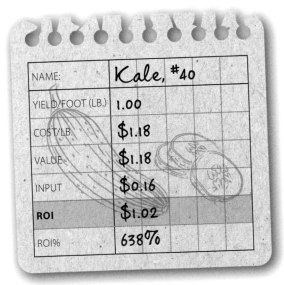

NAME:	Kale, #40
YIELD/FOOT (LB.)	1.00
COST/LB.	$1.18
VALUE	$1.18
INPUT	$0.16
ROI	$1.02
ROI%	638%

Value Added:

- Make sure your kale thrives by planting it with ideal partners. This leafy green will do well next to beets, herbs, onions, and potatoes, but shares nutrient needs with beans, strawberries, and tomatoes, so it should be planted away from these plants.

- Boost your kale yield by using seaweed mulch around the plants. The seaweed provides a burst of usable nutrition to the feeder roots lying just under the surface of the soil.

RADISH

Radishes are a favorite vegetable in the children's garden for the same reasons many adults love them: they are quick and easy. You can find radishes in shades of red and white, and even striped. But the real bonus for these bite-sized savory treats is that they only take about three weeks to mature.

For many gardeners, that means you have time to succession plant a second and sometimes a third crop (although you can also select carrot-shaped varieties). The crop will grow spring through early fall in most zones.

Plant seeds ½ inch deep in spring, and 1 inch deep in summer or early fall. If you experience fairly hot summers, you'll need to protect the growing plants. Afternoon shade, consistent watering, and a thick layer of mulch will give radishes the best chance to thrive under hot summer temperatures.

Keep the bed well weeded to prevent weed competition. Harvest the radishes when they are about the size of a jaw breaker, although they will be a bit sweeter if you harvest before they reach the mature size listed on the seed packet. As with just about everything else concerning radishes, harvesting is easy. Just pull the radish up, rinse clean, and refrigerate. Keep in mind that radish greens are every bit as edible as the root, and some people even think they are more delicious.

Value Added:

- Optimize the value you get out of your radish plot by planting more radishes every other week for a staggered but continuous harvest.

NAME:	Radish, #42		
YIELD/FOOT (LB.)	1.30		
COST/LB.	$1.15		
VALUE	$1.50		
INPUT	$0.48		
ROI	$1.02		
ROI%	211%		

BEET

Beets provide two beneficial crops in one. The bulb is incredibly useful in the kitchen serving as everything from a roasted side dish to a salad addition. Although the root is very nutritious, rich in phytonutrients that serve as antioxidants and alleviate inflammation, the greens are even more nutritious. Beet greens are ideal in a health shake, and can be steamed or sautéed as well.

Some varieties such as 'Bull's Blood' and 'Green Top' bunching beets are grown specifically for their greens. Others are meant specifically for putting up such as the early maturing 'Gladiator'. 'Golden' and 'Touchstone Gold' are gold colored with a mild, almost buttery flavor. Chioggia beets are striped inside, making a marvelous visual addition to the dinner table. You'll also find varieties meant for storing all winter, and even miniature bulbs.

No matter what type you're growing, beet seed pods contain multiple seeds. So you'll need to thin your seedlings if you're to harvest the plumpest beets possible.

Beets, like any root, require timing the harvest. Depending on variety, the growing period can be 45 to 60 days. Most cooks harvest slightly early—just when the shoulders of the beets become visible above the soil line. Although smaller, the beets will be more flavorful.

NAME:	Beet, #43
YIELD/FOOT (LB.)	1.00
COST/LB.	$1.86
VALUE	$1.86
INPUT	$0.85
ROI	$1.01
ROI%	119%

Value Added:

- Secure your investment—beets are favored by rabbits, deer, and other wildlife.

- Pickling is a classic way to preserve a larger harvest, and pickled beets are delicious all by themselves.

- Beets can be refrigerated for up to five days, but after that, flavor and firmness deteriorate rapidly.

ARTICHOKE

Artichokes won't grow well in all zones, but can be kept healthy and productive as far north as Zone 5. The trick is to provide a base of well-draining, highly nutritious, and moisture-retaining soil. Artichokes are thirsty and hungry plants and will probably need supplemental watering even if you're using a drip irrigation system. But they can die if waterlogged, so good drainage is key.

Artichokes are relatively pest and disease free. Snails and slugs sometimes attack young artichoke plants, but are easily combatted with any of a number of traps.

As with a few other perennial plants on this list, the true return on investment of artichokes needs to take into account the potential harvest over several years. A healthy plant can produce artichokes for five years, and the harvest will increase as the plant ages.

Each stem will typically produce more than one bud (artichoke). The top bud will ripen first. Harvest the buds before they open—check them carefully every day—when they are about the size of an apple. Cut the stems, leaving a few inches below the bud for ease of handling, and cook within a couple of days. Always handle artichokes carefully because they are prone to bruising.

Cut the stems to the ground in the fall to protect against insects. Cover the plants with a thick layer of mulch to help them overwinter (although they will not survive severe winters in any case).

Value Added:

- Want to grow a valuable crop in colder northern regions (Zones 5 and below)? You'll find a few artichoke varieties, such as 'Imperial Star' that were developed specifically to grow in colder climates.

NAME:	Artichoke, #44
YIELD/FOOT (LB.)	0.60
COST/LB.	$2.02
VALUE	$1.21
INPUT	$0.40
ROI	$0.81
ROI%	203%

CAULIFLOWER

This is a cool-weather plant like other members of the cabbage family. Unless your region experiences cool early summers, it's best to grow this vegetable exclusively in the fall.

Cauliflower does best in nutrient-rich soil, so ensure a good return on your investment by improving the soil prior to planting. You can also give the plants a boost with a dose of fish emulsion or compost tea every few weeks. You can avoid the danger of clubfoot disease or boron deficiency by avoiding plots where other cabbage family members were previously grown.

Make sure the leaves cover the head and protect it from direct sun exposure, which will yellow the cauliflower. Use a clothespin or rubber band to secure the leaves over the head, as necessary. This can make it hard to detect common pests, such as the cabbage worm. You can prevent insect infestation with a simple home remedy: Whisk together ½ cup of all-purpose flour with 1 tablespoon cayenne pepper, until thoroughly incorporated. Then dust the plants with the mixture and crawling insects will head for the hills.

To harvest a cauliflower, use a very sharp knife to cut the stem, leaving a few leaves around the base of the head.

Value Added:

- Don't make the mistake of thinking your cauliflower crop is a loss if your garden is hit by an early frost. Any unharvested heads will be fine for eating as long as they don't thaw and freeze again. Cut the frozen head and cook it immediately.

NAME:	Cauliflower, #45
YIELD/FOOT (LB.)	2.25
COST/LB.	$1.00
VALUE	$2.25
INPUT	$1.50
ROI	$0.75
ROI%	50%

SWEET POTATO

Sweet potatoes are not the most popular vegetable, but the rich flavor makes this a favorite among many gardeners who grow it. There are two types of sweet potato: moist and dry. Moist orange varieties are better known as "yams," but all varieties boast incredible flavor.

This isn't a hard plant to grow, but the vine does sprawl. That's usually not a problem because the foliage and the flowers are both quite attractive, so much so that the sweet potato is sometimes planted as a decorative border or groundcover.

Sweet potato plants don't require overly nutritious soil, but they do need a medium that drains well and is loose enough to allow tuber growth. For best success, plant "slips"—cut root sprouts available from nurseries and online sources. Put them in the soil in a sunny location about three weeks after the last frost.

Once the plants are established, cover the soil with black plastic or a thick layer of mulch. You can harvest the tubers when the vine leaves yellow, but the longer you wait, the larger and more nutritious they will be. Do not, however, leave them in the ground once the vine dies entirely, or you risk rot.

Dry your sweet potatoes in direct sun and then cure them for two weeks in a dark, well-ventilated location that is kept above 80 degrees Fahrenheit. Cure them completely and they'll stay good for months.

Value Added:
- Stay away from nitrogen-rich fertilizer. Too much nitrogen will boost leaf growth at the expense of the tubers, leading to a smaller harvest and lower value.

NAME:	Sweet Potato, #47
YIELD/FOOT (LB.)	2.00
COST/LB.	$0.82
VALUE	$1.64
INPUT	$1.02
ROI	$0.62
ROI%	61%

CELERY

There's no getting around the fact that celery can be a bit of a challenge to grow. But given how widely used it is in the kitchen, and the large yield from even 1 square foot of plants, many gardeners find it worth the effort.

Celery can take up to six months to mature. That's why most gardeners get a jump on the season by starting with a large-potted transplant rather than seed. The calculations here include that cost, but you can increase your return on investment by starting your plants indoors from seeds.

Celery needs highly nutritious, well-draining soil, and temperatures below 75 degrees Fahrenheit. Mulch well and water on a regular basis, supplying at least 1 inch per week.

Like cauliflower, celery can be "blanched" (protected from sun exposure) or not. Blanching can keep the celery from becoming bitter. Blanching entails covering the growing stalks up to the leaves—either with soil or a manufactured partition.

As the plant matures, you can cut off individual stalks as you need them in the kitchen, or you can harvest the whole plant at once by cutting it from the rootstock, right below the soil line.

NAME:	Celery, #49
YIELD/FOOT (LB.)	5.00
COST/LB.	$0.90
VALUE	$4.50
INPUT	$3.95
ROI	$0.55
ROI%	14%

Value Added:

- Want to see your return on investment soar with your next celery crop? Start your plants inside for free. Next time you buy celery, cut the base off the bunch and sit it in a deep saucer of water, so that bottom is submerged. Once new growth sprouts out of the center, plant the celery in the garden and *voila*: a new crop for free!

BEAN (BUSH AND POLE)

Beans are some of the easiest vegetable garden standards to grow and are also some of the most popular. However, their low produce-department price doesn't go far in rewarding even the modest effort it takes to grow the plants.

If you're conflicted about which type of bean to plant, consider your space constraints and flavor. The vertical growth of pole beans are a plus where space is at a premium and most people find pole beans the more flavorful of the two.

You can also add visual interest to the garden and a different flavor to the table by planting a yellow wax bean, such as 'Monte Gusto' or a purple bean, like 'Purple King'.

Although certain varieties of French beans and all "yard-longs" are meant to grow from 10 to 18 inches long, bigger is usually not necessarily better with this crop. Pick the beans when they are full-size and ripe, but do not let them get so big that they look about to burst. Harvest the beans carefully to avoid damaging the plant. Cut or snap the stem holding the bean to the plant. Remove beans as soon as they are ripe to keep the plant productive as long into the season as possible, and to maximize your output and your investment.

Value Added:

- Get extra value out of your bean plantings by planting at least one scarlet runner bean plant. Not only will you be adding a beautiful splash of color to your edible garden, scarlet runner beans attract bumblebees and hummingbirds to the garden.

NAME:	Bean, Bush, #50	Bean, Pole, #51
YIELD/FOOT (LB.)	0.50	0.40
COST/LB.	$1.36	$1.36
VALUE	$0.68	$0.54
INPUT	$0.79	$0.94
ROI	−$0.11	−$0.40
ROI%	−14%	−42%

OKRA

Although considered a southern heat-loving crop, you can plant this vegetable in cooler northern gardens. The trick is to start from well-established seedlings, planted out as soon as the nights reach 60 degrees Fahrenheit or more on a regular basis. Grow your crop from seeds instead of mature seedlings and you'll turn a net negative value into a positive value with a return on investment of over 1,000 percent.

However, transplanting okra is a delicate operation. Damage to the young taproot will kill the plant, so you have to handle the seedling as if it were made of glass. The plants require full sun and, although drought tolerant, they'll do best with a steady supply of water—at least 1 inch per week.

Okra grows lovely yellow flowers, which then produce the edible pods. Pods must be regularly harvested before they overmature to ensure that the plant continues producing. Begin taking the pods when they reach about 4 inches long. Use pruning shears to cut each pod off the stem.

Okra features a natural defense system of tiny, bristly hairs. Some people experience an allergic reaction to these, and most gardeners will experience at least some irritation after brushing up against them. Always wear gloves and a long-sleeved shirt when working with okra plants.

Value Added:
- Although the return on investment is negligible if you're starting from seedlings, you may want to plant okra anyway. The vegetable is a great disease fighter, credited with playing a role in preventing several forms of cancer and combating heart disease and high cholesterol.

NAME:	Okra, #52
YIELD/FOOT (LB.)	1.00
COST/LB.	$3.25
VALUE	$3.25
INPUT	$3.95
ROI	-$0.70
ROI%	-18%

ASPARAGUS

These plants cannot be harvested until they have grown for two or three years. Fortunately, you don't have to wait that long because you can buy two- or three-year-old plant roots called "crowns," which have been grown in nurseries. You usually still have to give them one year of growth in your garden before the first limited harvest. After that, full harvest ahead. Calculating the value of asparagus from your garden can be tricky business. However, you can start asparagus from seed, in which case the input number above would change to $0.27, and your return on investment would be 19%. In either case, you always want to plant male plants. Plant crowns in spring, after the soil has warmed. Keep your asparagus happy with lots of compost or composted manure, including sidedressing during the season.

But the most important point to keep in mind is that unlike the most of the other crops on this list, asparagus is perennial and will provide a crop for years after the first harvest—the plants can actually produce for more than a decade. You must ensure that the bed is properly tended because asparagus will suffer greatly if competing with even a few weeds. Although the square foot measure works the same whether you're growing in rows or squares, you can crowd square sections of raised beds with up to four plants instead of the recommended one, greatly increasing your yield (and your ROI).

Choose varieties bred in New Jersey, such as 'Jersey Giant', for maximum productivity and disease resistance.

Value Added:
- Good practices will maximize your yield. Cut the largest shoots right at the surface of the soil as cleanly as possible, using a serrated knife and a slanting cut. Don't let your asparagus spears get larger than 6 inches, or they will become tough.

NAME:	Asparagus, #53
YIELD/FOOT (LB.)	0.10
COST/LB.	$3.17
VALUE	$0.32
INPUT	$1.22
ROI	-$0.90
ROI%	-74%

SWISS CHARD

Swiss chard is pretty enough to grow in a decorative foliage border and hardy enough to straddle the divide between cool-weather and hot-weather crops. Although it's not rugged enough to hold up to long-distance transport, it's strong enough to grow deeper into summer than most other greens and will tolerate a light frost in fall. Add in the fact that it's a powerhouse of nutrients as well, and you have a leafy green that's attractive in more ways than one.

Plant mature seedlings in the garden about two weeks before your last spring frost date (or about ten weeks before the first frost date in fall). Ensure good air circulation because fungal diseases can be a problem. The plant needs well-drained soil, but a constant supply of water.

Slugs can be a problem because they love Swiss chard leaves every bit as much as humans do, but they are easily stymied with a beer-and-saucer trap or by sprinkling sawdust or coarse rock dust around the base of each plant.

As with most greens, you can start harvesting Swiss chard leaves once they reach about 6 inches tall. Younger leaves have a sweeter, richer flavor and will be noticeably more tender than mature leaves. Compost or discard older leaves that no longer have a sheen.

Value Added:

- If you're lucky enough to live in a temperate zone that isn't subjected to a hard freeze in winter, your Swiss chard may act like a perennial. When the plant bolts, cut the head off the root stalk and it will produce more leaves.

NAME:	Swiss Chard, #54
YIELD/FOOT (LB.)	6.00
COST/LB.	$1.95
VALUE	$11.70
INPUT	$13.32
ROI	-$1.62
ROI%	-12%

BELL PEPPER

Bell peppers are one of the core mainstays of produce aisles everywhere because the plant is so easy to grow and adapts well to greenhouse culture for year-round production. Green peppers are the less-mature versions of yellow and red, and are consequently not as sweet or flavorful. For a wonderful look in the garden and on the table, grow brilliantly colored varieties such as 'Orange Blaze' or the dark purple 'Sweet Chocolate Belle'.

Color is also an indication of nutrients in the pepper. Red peppers are especially rich sources of disease-fighting carotenoid phytonutrients, while any color other than green is dense with vitamins A and C and beta carotene.

You'll find that bell peppers are exceptionally well suited to container gardening. No matter where they are grown, you'll make the most of your harvest by staking the plant.

You won't need to worry much about pests or diseases, but protect plants from inclement weather by covering them if you experience a late spring cold spell. Use pruning shears to cut mature bell pepper stems; pulling the peppers off the plant can damage branches and lower productivity. If your peppers have just started to change color when you harvest them, keep them at room temperature for two to three days and they will continue to ripen.

Value Added:

- On a pure value basis, waiting a little longer to let bell pepper fruits mature makes sense because at retail, colored varieties are from 50 to 100 percent more expensive.

NAME:	Bell Pepper, #55
YIELD/FOOT (LB.)	2.00
COST/LB.	$1.50
VALUE	$3.00
INPUT	$4.90
ROI	-$1.90
ROI%	-39%

BRUSSELS SPROUTS

Belonging to the same family as cabbage and broccoli, Brussels sprouts prefer the same mist-cooled environment as those plants. Generally planted in fall, the plant may tolerate an early spring planting in cooler parts of the country. The plant takes so long to mature (generally around 80 days) that most gardeners choose to purchase and plant transplants because growing from seed is not feasible. You can, however, change the ROI picture for this crop if you start your own transplants inside and plant them out in the garden immediately after any danger of frost has passed. The seeds for a single plant will reduce the input cost to less than two cents.

The plants are susceptible to a range of diseases, soil deficiencies, and pests, so it's wise to pay close attention to the health of the plant by inspecting the leaves and stems every couple of days.

Harvest the plant from top to bottom, cutting off the sprouts when they are about 1 inch in diameter and still firm and tight. Some home gardeners remove the leaves of the plant to speed up the harvest.

NAME:	Brussels Sprouts, #56
YIELD/FOOT (LB.)	0.40
COST/LB.	$2.72
VALUE	$1.09
INPUT	$4.90
ROI	-$3.81
ROI%	-78%

Value Added:

- Get the most out of each Brussels sprouts plant by cleaning and cooking the leaves of the plant as you would collard greens or using the leaves in green smoothies. The leaves contain abundant nutrients.

- Don't wash Brussels sprouts before storing; wait until you're about to cook them to trim, clean, and wash them.

- Don't panic if a frost hits your fall crop of Brussels sprouts; a frost can accentuate the sweetness in the sprouts.

Russet

POTATO (RUSSET, YELLOW, RED)

For such a basic sustenance crop, potatoes offer an incredibly diverse bounty. You can certainly choose to grow plain old Russets, but the possibilities go far beyond dull brown tubers. You'll find potatoes in a rainbow of colors, from white to purple, and a range of shapes as well. 'Midnight Moon' is a stunning red potato that is actually deep purple, and 'Adirondack Blue' is deep blue through and through. 'Masquerade' is a mottled purple and white, and French fingerlings boast fun shapes it's hard not to love.

A primary source of starch and fiber, potatoes can be prepared in any number of ways, from deep-frying to baking. Regardless of which variety you choose and how you want to prepare them, potatoes are an easy crop to grow. However, keep in mind that potatoes are a true cool-season crop; summer heat is a growing potato's enemy.

Potatoes are their own seed source. Instead of planting seeds, plant your own seed sprouts. (Use only certified, disease-free seed potatoes.) Sprout them in a tray a week before planting. Then cut pieces, each including an eye, and plant them in a deep hole with the eye facing up. Cover with a healthy sprinkling of soil. The soil has to be at least 50 degrees Fahrenheit when you do this, or you risk infection of the seeds.

When sprouts appear, cover with soil and continue the process until the potatoes send up flower stalks and begin to flower. When the potatoes show signs of flowering, increase the amount of water, apply a thick layer of mulch, and let the flowers bloom.

Open flowers are the sign that the potatoes are ready to harvest. As soon as the flowers begin to die, loosen the soil around the potatoes and dig them up.

Value Added:
- Get a design bonus out of your potatoes by growing them in an ornamental border or flowerbed. The white flowers most potatoes send up are simply stunning.

- Avoid wasting your effort with supermarket potatoes. Many are treated with

Yellow

Red

chemicals to inhibit sprouting and you can't be sure these potatoes are disease-free.

- If you haven't completely covered a sprouting potato, the potato will turn green. Discard green potatoes because the flavor will be off and the potato will actually be mildly toxic.

NAME:	Potato, Russet, #57	Potato, Yellow, #58	Potato, Red, #59
YIELD/FOOT (LB.)	4.00	2.00	2.00
COST/LB.	$0.90	$1.01	$0.88
VALUE	$3.60	$2.02	$1.76
INPUT	$7.98	$7.98	$7.98
ROI	−$4.38	−$5.96	−$6.22
ROI%	−55%	−75%	−78%

VEGGIES IN ALPHABETICAL ORDER

VEGGIE	RANK	PAGE	VEGGIE	RANK	PAGE
ASPARAGUS	53	87	MUSTARD GREENS	11	54
ARTICHOKE	44	81	OKRA	52	86
ARUGULA	15	60	ONION, RED	20	55
BASIL	1	39	ONION, WHITE	18	55
BEAN, BUSH	50	85	ONION, YELLOW	12	55
BEAN, POLE	51	85	OREGANO	1	40
BEET	43	80	PARSLEY, CURLY	1	44
BELL PEPPER	55	89	PARSLEY, FLAT-LEAF	1	44
BROCCOLI	36	76	PARSNIP	2	46
BRUSSELS SPROUTS	56	90	PEA, SUGAR SNAP	38	77
CABBAGE, GREEN	48	74	PEA, SNOW	41	77
CABBAGE, NAPA	37	74	POTATO, RED	59	91
CABBAGE, RED	46	74	POTATO, RUSSET	57	91
CABBAGE, SAVOY	35	74	POTATO, YELLOW	58	91
CANTALOUPE	30	69	PUMPKIN	13	57
CARROT, HEIRLOOM	31	70	RADICCHIO	26	65
CARROT, HYBRID	39	70	RADISH	42	79
CAULIFLOWER	45	82	RADISH, DAIKON	32	71
CELERY	49	84	ROSEMARY	1	35
CHIVES	1	37	SAGE	1	42
CILANTRO	1	43	SPINACH	9	53
COLLARD GREENS	33	72	SQUASH, WINTER	8	52
CORN	34	73	STRAWBERRY	23	63
CUCUMBER	16	61	SWEET POTATO	47	83
DILL	1	41	SWISS CHARD	54	88
EGGPLANT	29	68	TARRAGON, FRENCH	1	38
FENNEL (BULB)	28	67	THYME	1	34
GARLIC	4	49	TOMATO, CHERRY	3	47
KALE	40	78	TOMATO, HEIRLOOM	5	47
KOHLRABI	27	66	TOMATO, HYBRID	10	47
LEEK	7	51	TOMATO, ROMA	19	47
LETTUCE, BUTTER	25	58	TURNIP	6	50
LETTUCE, GREEN/ RED LEAF	22	58	WATERMELON	21	62
LETTUCE, MESCLUN	14	58	ZUCCHINI, SUMMER SQUASH	24	64
LETTUCE, ROMAINE	17	58			
MINT	1	36			

SECTION 3

OTHER KINDS OF VALUE

Obviously, there are many different ways of looking at value. If you're like most gardeners, you see value in the garden far beyond the pure profit-and-loss picture presented by the listings in Section 2. There are actually many types of value gardeners can enjoy from the garden. That's why, when it comes to discussing true garden value, you have to consider what matters most to you and your family. If it truly is getting the best monetary return on your investment, then boosting the production of your garden as much as possible is key.

10 MOST BEAUTIFUL EDIBLES FOR AN ORNAMENTAL GARDEN — PAGE 96

10 HEALTHIEST VEGETABLES TO GROW — PAGE 98

10 BEST VEGETABLES FOR A CHILD'S GARDEN — PAGE 100

10 BEST VEGETABLES FOR GRILLING — PAGE 102

10 BEST VEGETABLES FOR CONTAINERS — PAGE 104

10 BEST VEGETABLES FOR A FASCINATION GARDEN — PAGE 106

10 MOST POPULAR VEGETABLE SEEDS — PAGE 108

10 BEST VEGETABLES FOR CHALLENGING SOILS — PAGE 110

10 BEST VEGETABLES FOR WEIGHT LOSS — PAGE 112

10 BEST VEGETABLES FOR OVERALL YIELDS — PAGE 114

10 BEST EDIBLE FLOWERS — PAGE 116

10 FASTEST-GROWING VEGETABLES — PAGE 118

10 BEST EDIBLES FOR SHADY GARDENS — PAGE 120

10 MOST BEAUTIFUL
EDIBLES FOR AN
ORNAMENTAL GARDEN

Increase the value of garden edibles by choosing plants to do double duty, supplying beauty as well as nutrition. Exploiting the aesthetic potential in edibles is all a matter of picking the right varietals and using them in an enlightened way, according to **Shawna Coronado**, author of *Grow a Living Wall: Create Vertical Gardens with Purpose*. "The number-one requirement of an ornamental edible is that it be full of color. For instance, a blood beet grows stunning greens in bold burgundy—a fantastic show in the garden. Second is structure. Dinosaur kale is a great plant for decorative gardens because it has a fantastic and unique structure. You can incorporate it into a formal design or do something very casual with it, and it will still look great."

Coronado also believes that the right edible can be a showstopper on its own, as a specimen plant. "I love 'Ruby Perfection' cabbage. It has a burgundy-blue, almost purple tint. The color is bold, but the cabbage is also shaped like a giant flower. Use it as a specimen plant or as an isolated feature in a decorative garden and it really shines."

Whether you're seamlessly integrating edibles into a bed or border, or just hoping to keep a vegetable garden looking its best, Coronado recommends a very simple strategy. "I constantly keep a pruner in my hand every time I walk outside into the garden and I snip a couple snips. It's just a matter of keeping the brown bits trimmed up. It's also essential to water well so that you're not losing leaves to dryness and wilting."

Coronado's favorite edibles for a decorative garden include:

1	**SWISS CHARD** **(BETA VULGARIS** **'BRIGHT LIGHTS')**	'Bright Lights' has gorgeous red, orange, yellow, and white stems that melt my heart. The brilliant stems hold dramatically dark red and green leaves. My favorite way to prepare Swiss chard is to eat it raw in salads with olive oil and vinegar.
2	**BASIL** **(OCIMUM BASILICUM** **'SPICY GLOBE')**	A beautiful globe shape, great flavor, and a powerful scent are why I line my garden beds with this herb. Once the Spicy Globe basil fills in all around the borders of the garden, not a single rabbit steps inside. It's a wonderfully wildlife-resistant plant.
3	**MINT** **(MENTHA* PIPERITA** **F. CITRATA** **'CHOCOLATE')**	Chocolate mint is perhaps the most heavenly smelling mint in existence and has a stunning form. It spills beautifully out of containers. It is invasive, but plant it in a container and sit it right next to your patio and you will be rewarded with an amazing, scented outdoor room.
4	**KALE** **(BRASSICA** **OLERACEA** **'DINOSAUR' OR** **'NERO DI TOSCANA')**	Dinosaur kale is one of the strongest blues in the ornamental edible world. It is also incredibly nutritious. It works brilliantly as a tall thriller in the middle of a container, or plant a bed of them for a huge blue wave. Kale is simply perfect in casseroles, with eggs, or sautéed alone as a side dish.
5	**CABBAGE** **(BRASSICA** **OLERACEA** **[CAPITATA GROUP]** **'RUBY PERFECTION')**	When I first laid eyes on 'Ruby Perfection' I knew I was in love. The plant looks like a giant burgundy flower. Though planting them in rows is pretty, they have a stunning impact as a garden focal point. Cabbage tastes remarkably delicious when used to make chipotle slaw for tacos.
6	**CURLY** **PARSLEY** **(PETROSELINUM** **CRISPUM VAR.** **CRISPUM)**	Curly parsley is what I call a "surprise plant." It has this fantastic way of filling in all the nooks and crannies in a container or bed with its bright green color and curly form.
7	**PEPPER** **(CAPSICUM ANNUUM** **'SANGRIA')**	I grew 'Sangria' for its peppers and was delighted by its form—short, round, and loaded with long, pointed, purple and red peppers. Ornamental peppers are popular right now, but most are so hot that gardeners don't eat them. Sangria has a lower Scoville rating and is a mild pepper great for guacamole or for hanging as decoration.
8	**BULL'S BLOOD** **BEET** **(BETA VULGARIS** **'BULL'S BLOOD')**	'Bull's Blood' beets and greens are the most fabulous shade of deep burgundy, and I love to use the greens in the summer salads I make. They can be grown for the leaf in shade or part shade. Grow a larger root by placing the plant in full sun. Bull's Blood makes a great "filler" in container gardens.
9	**ROSEMARY** **(ROSMARINUS** **OFFICINALIS)**	In warmer regions, rosemary grows into delicious shrubs that smell wonderful and are quite attractive. Flowering rosemary attracts native bees and makes a very striking display. It prefers a drier environment and tastes as good as it smells.
10	**CHIVE** **(ALLIUM** **SCHOENOPRASUM)**	Chives are a cool-season perennial that can be used all season long for cooking, while serving as a lovely ornamental. Chives' round flowers on tall stems blooms for several weeks, and are the stars of my early season garden.

10 HEALTHIEST
VEGETABLES TO GROW

There are several ways to measure the health benefits of any vegetable. That's why different medical authorities might change the order of any Top-10 list. The list here includes nutritional powerhouses that, although they might be placed in a different order, would probably find a place on anybody's Top-10 list.

It's important to keep in mind that no vegetable is a silver bullet to disease. The best diet is well rounded and includes a mix of many different vegetables, and ideally, a rainbow of colors. The more important point is that you eat enough vegetables. Studies show that less than half of Americans are eating the USDA recommended minimum of five servings of fruits and vegetables a day (a serving is generally described as ½ cup of raw fruits or vegetables). So the first step toward a healthier future may simply be increasing the amount of vegetables you consume—including as many as possible from this list.

Choosing the vegetables is only the first step in getting the most nutrients you can out them. How you prepare and consume those vegetables is also essential to how many usable nutrients your body takes from what it consumes. Start with organic vegetables free of the chemicals and additives often found in non-organic options.

Fermenting: This age-old process of preserving food creates essential microbes that can help balance intestinal flora and clear your system of toxins. Most vegetables can be fermented. It's a great way to put up a large harvest.

Juicing: Juicing does what our modern teeth often fail to do: crush vegetables so well that locked-in nutrients are freed and made available to the small intestine. Juiced vegetables are a way to get many servings of vegetables in a compact, quickly consumable form.

Cooking: The trick is to use a variety of cooking methods for best results with vegetables. Some nutrients can be killed by the high heat of roasting or sautéing, while others are released only when the vegetable is heated.

1	**BROCCOLI**	This hearty green vegetable boasts an unusual combination of phytonutrients that help detox the body, abundant vitamin A and K that can help with vitamin D synthesis, and a flavonoid that acts as an anti-inflammatory. Boost the cholesterol-lowering properties of broccoli by steaming it.
2	**KALE**	One of the first vegetables to be touted as a superfood, kale contains alpha-lipoic acid, which studies have shown to lower glucose levels and improve other factors contributing to diabetic damage in the body. Rich in a range of vitamins, fiber, and minerals such as potassium, kale has been linked to reduced risk of certain types of cancer, heart disease, stroke, and even kidney stones.
3	**SPINACH**	Popeye was right! Spinach—particularly the darkest green leaves—contains carotenoids that play a role in eye health and preventing macular degeneration. Cooking the greens makes the specific carotenoid lutein more available to your body. Preliminary research suggests that *glycoglycerolipids* found in spinach may protect the digestive tract lining and reduce inflammation.
4	**CABBAGE**	Both red and green varieties not only contain compounds associated with preventing cancer, they also include some that have been shown to moderate the effects of radiation therapy. *Anthocyanins* in red cabbage have been linked to inflammation reduction and may play a role in fighting heart disease. Fermented forms are particular potent in spurring digestive and immune system health.
5	**COLLARD GREENS**	In addition to being a key source of vitamin K, collard greens supply impressive amounts of minerals including folate, thiamin, niacin, pantothenic acid, choline, phosphorus, and potassium. Collard greens, along with other green vegetables, have cancer-fighting properties and have been shown to counteract the carcinogenic compounds in some grilled foods.
6	**BRUSSELS SPROUTS**	Brussels sprouts boast many of the same benefits associated with other cruciferous vegetables but have some of the highest levels of cancer-preventing *glucosinolates*. It is essential that you not overcook Brussels sprouts, because overcooking destroys much of the vegetable's nutrient power. Steam or roast the sprouts to an *al dente* texture only.
7	**BEET**	Pickle, roast, or serve them raw, these roots are high in cancer-preventing antioxidants. They also contain lutein, a compound that aids eye health. The vegetable is actually a two-for-one because the leaves are even more packed with a variety of nutrients than the roots are. Cook them as you would spinach, or use them in a green smoothie.
8	**SUGAR SNAP PEA**	These solid performers should be eaten with the pods intact for maximum benefit. Steam them or eat them raw, and you'll enjoy a fiber-rich food that delivers high amounts of vitamins C and A—valuable antioxidants. These garden treats also offer good amounts of iron and manganese.
9	**PEPPER**	The sweeter bell peppers contain lots of vitamin C and loads of fiber. Hotter peppers often have higher levels of *capsaicin*, a compound that has been linked to lowering cholesterol, helping control diabetes, and reducing inflammation in the body.
10	**SQUASH (SUMMER AND WINTER)**	It's hard to think of squash as one vegetable, because it has so many faces—from summer's zucchini to winter's butternut. But all are excellent sources of fiber, contain immune system-boosting and anti-inflammatory compounds, and are rich in nutrients such as alpha and beta-carotenes, which keep your eyes healthy.

10 BEST VEGETABLES FOR A CHILD'S GARDEN

Sharon Lovejoy has worked with enough children in the garden to know what captures youngsters' attention and what leaves them yearning for a TV. The author of *Roots, Shoots, Buckets & Boots: Gardening Together with Children* and host of her own fun-packed website, www.sharonlovejoy.com, Lovejoy believes you have to make the garden both manageable and fascinating for young green thumbs to come into their own. As she puts it, "It's more about the love factor and personality than anything else." She has developed a few tried-and-true strategies for keeping kids interested from planting through harvest.

Containerize: Kids can view long, straight rows under a hot sun as work and drudgery rather than fun. That's why Lovejoy suggests corralling plants into kid-friendly growing spaces. "It's really easy for kids to grow vegetables in half-barrels, wooden produce boxes, and other containers. It makes sense because they're not tending a huge garden area. Instead, you put all the energy and finances into one little space."

Foster connection: In addition to placing containers where children can watch their garden grow, Lovejoy recommends using smaller gardening accessories. "Keep a kid-sized watering can handy. I love to say, 'Hey check out your plants and see if they're thirsty. And remember that they're the opposite of us, they want their toes watered!'" She also suggests keeping a colander or basket in the garden for harvesting.

Make it fun: Lovejoy advocates involving children at every step in the gardening adventure. "Take your children to the garden center or look through a catalog with them. Catalogs are full of fun options." She suggests picking unusual colors, shapes, and textures to really intrigue children. "Kids love when things are called one thing but look like something else."

Here is Lovejoy's Top 10, and her comments about each:

1 PUMPKIN

Kids just love pumpkin. They can grow a giant pumpkin in an old garbage can with screened drainage holes. As an alternative, help your child grow spaghetti squash—a fun and nutritious substitute for pasta night.

2 CORN

Corn is so easy to grow, and kids can choose from such a wide variety. They love to grow their own popping corn. You can even plant beautiful strawberry popping corn.

3 BEAN

I adore scarlet runner beans and painted lady beans for kids. Both have flowers that are edible and form wonderful seedpods. Their speckled beans are great for soup. The plants also attract hummingbirds.

4 CARROT

Don't grow plain carrots. Kids can choose purple or a fun mini like 'Thumbelina'. These are underground treasures; children just love to pull them out of the ground.

5 RADISH

This is probably the easiest plant to grow in a child's garden. I'd suggest trying unusual varieties like 'French Breakfast', 'White Icicle', or 'Black Spanish'. But probably the favorite of kids everywhere is 'Easter Eggs' because they come in a wonderful rainbow of pastel colors.

6 TOMATO

Children like to grow tomatoes, and the plant is so adaptable to containers. I like green grape and red grape, or pear tomatoes, and I have kids grow the tiny currant tomatoes. It's best to choose indeterminate varieties so that kids can pick them—and eat them—all summer long.

7 WATERMELON

Right now my grandson is growing watermelons, and he's crazy about them. If you really want to capture and captivate children, grow 'Moon and Stars'. They have a big moon and constellations all over the rind. Just lovely.

8 POTATO

Something I always grow with kids is a tub of taters. I like 'Ruby Crescents', yellow fingerlings, and 'Yukon Gold'. Go for blue and purple varieties, which are high in vitamins and minerals.

9 LETTUCE

Get all different kinds. Frisee, deer tongue—they all taste great. Plant them like a bouquet. Kids love that. Sprinkle in some kale. Children especially like butter lettuce and Romaine.

10 CUCUMBER

I like all cucumbers, and they're all good, but 'Lemon' is especially wonderful. Kids are fascinated that it's shaped like a lemon, colored like a lemon, but it's a cucumber inside.

10 BEST VEGETABLES FOR GRILLING

Grilled veggies are the perfect way to round out any barbecue cookout. From simply grilling burgers for a Saturday light lunch, to a full-blown outdoor Sunday social with true barbecued brisket, vegetables add a multitude of flavors and a bit more nutrition to your backyard feasts. Grilled vegetables are also your way to accommodate vegetarians in a cookout, but don't forget that you can grill veggies any day of the week with the help of a simple non-stick grill pan.

The best vegetables for grilling are those that respond to heat by producing enhanced flavors. Sometimes, such as with onions, its about caramelizing the natural sugars in the vegetable. Other times, such as with radicchio, it's about mellowing out an overly strong flavor so that it becomes something more pleasant and mild.

The one cardinal sin in grilling, whether you've got a protein over the flames or are cooking vegetarian, is to burn the food. Keep a close eye on the grill when you're grilling vegetables because they can burn or turn overly mushy in the blink of an eye when flipped onto an unexpected hot spot.

One of the great uses of grilling is to rescue vegetables that are a day past their prime. If you've just collected a large harvest all at one time, you can grill some of the extra and the refrigerate it. Most grilled vegetables will keep for up to a week if refrigerated, and they can be incorporated into everything from eggs to rice casseroles to cold salads with a little feta.

1	**EGGPLANT**	As with most vegetables, simple is best when grilling this purple crowd-pleaser. Cut an eggplant into ½-thick slices, coat each slice with olive oil, sprinkle with Kosher salt and fresh ground pepper, and grill on medium-high heat for about 4 minutes per side. Most grillers undercook eggplant; it should be soft and gray.
2	**ONION**	It's best to grill onion wedges rather than slices because this will be keep the onions together—slices can fall apart into rings. All onions need is a light coating of olive oil and they're ready to grill. Grill for about 17 minutes covered by a foil pan. Turn the wedges once or twice with tongs. Yellow and white onions are fine for grilling, but red onions become incredibly sweet when grilled and are simply heavenly.
3	**RADICCHIO**	You might not think this salad addition could hold up to grilling, but you'd be wrong. Slice a head into wedges along the length, including a portion of the stem with each wedge. Coat with olive oil and a sprinkle of sea salt, and then grill over medium-high heat for 10 minutes with the lid closed.
4	**ZUCCHINI**	For a pleasingly mild, smoky flavor, it's hard to top grilled zucchini slices. Slice a zucchini lengthwise into thin slices. Melt a quarter stick of butter and whisk in the juice of a one lemon and half a teaspoon of oregano, and brush the slices liberally. Grill over medium heat for about 10 minutes on one side, flip, and grill on the other for about 3 minutes. The slices should be tender but still slightly firm, with char marks.
5	**BRUSSELS SPROUTS**	This may not be the first vegetable that pops to mind when you think of grilling, but the sublime flavor when grilled makes this one well worth considering. Whisk together olive oil, a splash of Dijon mustard, minced garlic, and some salt and pepper. Clean, trim, and coat the Brussels sprouts with the marinade and then skewer the sprouts. Grill over medium heat for 5 minutes, then flip and cook for 5 minutes more.
6	**CORN**	Corn on the cob is so delicious grilled that once you try it once, you'll probably never cook it any other way. You can grill it in the husk or the bare ear wrapped in foil. If the corn is in the husk, soak in water for about 10 minutes before grilling. If it's in foil, add a pat of butter to each ear. Grill either way, turning occasionally, for 20 minutes over medium heat.
7	**POTATO**	All kinds of potatoes can be grilled, for a flavor much like roasted potatoes. Many cooks parboil the potatoes for 10 minutes, although many grillers just grill the potatoes longer, watching them closely. Grill slices or red potato halves by coating them with oil, dusting with chopped fresh rosemary, and sprinkling with sea salt. Grill 3 to 4 minutes on each side, until deeply scarred by char marks and fork tender.
8	**TOMATO**	Tomatoes are an unusual grilled veggie that really brings something special to a cookout. Slice a large hybrid like a beefsteak into thick slices. Brush with olive oil and grill for about 5 minutes without turning. Make the tomatoes extra special by grilling with a dollop of pesto or olive tapenade on top of the tomato.
9	**BELL PEPPER**	Grilled bell peppers have a smoky roasted quality to them that makes them ideal accompaniments to grilled meat and pork. Clean, seed, and trim the peppers and cut them into halves. Coat with olive oil and grill on one side for about 5 minutes and the second side for about 3 minutes, allowing the skin to char.
10	**ASPARAGUS**	Asparagus is wonderful grilled with just a coating of olive oil or wrapped in bacon and grilled until the bacon is done. In either case, use thicker varieties, or use a grilling basket to stop thinner stems from slipping through grill grates.

10 BEST VEGETABLES FOR CONTAINERS

Containers can be an incredibly efficient way to grow edibles, whether you're using them to supplement a larger backyard garden or as a standalone garden. The beauty of containers is that you control all aspects of cultivation. It's easier to know what's in the soil, and simpler to detect and deal with problems such as pests and diseases as soon as they arise.

Containers are also mobile. This means you can move them to match the sun, adjusting for trees that leaf out over the season, or just for the movement of the sun in the sky over the course of a season, or as seasons change. You can even move sensitive crops indoors as need be—a great way to extend the growing season with a container garden.

That said, you should be careful when selecting containers for edibles. Some materials, such as the ubiquitous terra cotta, have drawbacks that may not serve vegetables well. For instance, unfinished terra cotta may leach water too quickly away from thirsty plants roots. Wood containers may have contained substances that left behind compounds harmful to plant roots. It pays to be careful about the containers you use.

You should also take the opportunity of choosing containers to find ones that suit the look of your backyard (or front yard, as the case may be). Containers can be an excellent way to beautify your outdoor spaces, and you can always paint or otherwise modify your containers to improve the style.

1	**HERBS**	If you're going to consume large amounts of the herbs you grow, such as basil, dedicating one container to a plant makes sense. However, if you're looking for a small kitchen garden, you can use a larger container such as a half-barrel to grow smaller amounts assortment of your favorite herbs all in one place.
2	**TOMATO**	Tomatoes thrive on controlled water, making containers ideal because you can easily check soil moisture and provide a consistent supply of water with drip irrigation or even a small hand-watering cup. Most will grow up inside a tomato cage quite handily, allowing for excellent air circulation and perfect positioning for ideal sunlight exposure.
3	**BUSH BEAN**	Bush bean plants fill out the average large container and leave room for a support if necessary. Container planting also makes it easy to check for any pests and to harvest your crop when it's ready.
4	**POTATO**	Use a large, deep container, and continue covering the emerging sprouts with soil and you'll wind up with a bumper crop of spuds. A container will also allow you to make sure there is nothing in the soil—disease or pest—that might attack the growing roots.
5	**EGGPLANT**	Use a trellis in a large container to grow eggplants up a support, offering them beneficial air circulation, ideal sun exposure, and easy harvesting.
6	**BELL PEPPER**	Bell peppers—and other pepper plants for that matter—are ideal container plants. The bush will thrive and the container can be moved to the shade when the heat threatens to overwhelm the plant.
7	**SWISS CHARD**	This is an ideal crop for a medium-sized container (a recycled 5-gallon bucket is ideal). This will accommodate the plant's taproot and allow for a bushy top growth. Place the bucket right outside the kitchen door so that you can harvest leaves whenever you want to.
8	**RADISH**	Radishes are ideal for a child's container garden. Use multicolored varieties to introduce children to the wonders of gardening and show them how to care for plants in a confined, easily manageable area.
9	**LETTUCE**	Use a large container and grow a salad garden. Mix and match different types of lettuce. An all-in-one container will allow you to snip as you go and make custom salads from whatever happens to be ripe. It will also keep the tasty greens out of the reach of snails and slugs.
10	**SPINACH**	The rich, healthy, nutrient-packed greens do best in super-nutritious soil, which you can provide in one easy package by planting in a container. You can also keep this useful kitchen standard growing for as long as possible by keeping it in the sun and moving it inside to extend the season.

10 BEST VEGETABLES FOR A FASCINATION GARDEN

Introducing a little oddity into the edible garden is a terrific way to add interest, expand your culinary horizons and experiment in the backyard. In addition to the list below, a little investigation in seed catalogs will turn up eye-popping unusual varieties of standard vegetables.

Fascination plantings don't necessarily have to take up a large amount of your valuable garden real estate; planting a couple of these can add more than their fair share of interest. Many, such as black radishes or 'Green Zebra' tomatoes, are also just as productive and useful for eating purposes as their more commonplace relatives.

Unusual plantings are an excellent way to get children engaged and involved in gardening. The weirder, the better. The more they see strange things grow—plants that pique their curiosity—the more they'll want to grow. And kids aren't alone. Weird vegetables can be a way for any gardener to amuse herself or himself and any visitors to the garden. This part of the garden can also add a lot of interest to a cookout or outdoor cocktail party. Some of these are great conversation starters.

You can eat all of these, but they may not be to everyone's taste. Regardless, be sure to learn all can about the cultivation of any plant on this list, because some require specialized care to grow their best.

1	**MEXICAN SOUR GHERKIN CUCUMBER**	If any vegetable can be described as adorable, this is the one. The prolific plant produces 1-inch long fruit that look remarkably like miniature watermelons. The flavor is pure fresh cucumber with a hint of citrus. Kids will absolutely love these plants.
2	**ROMANESCO BROCCOLI**	If broccoli grew on Mars, this is what it would look like. Resembling the drill head for machines that bore through mountains, the spiral, conical form competes with the glow-in-the-dark lime green color for attention. However, it's delicious and can be prepared in exactly the same way as any other broccoli.
3	**PURPLE KOHLRABI**	Kohlrabi is yet another vegetable that looks like a space being with antennas. The green variety looks otherworldly enough, but in an intriguing shade of light purple it looks downright weird. A relative of cabbage, even the purple variety can be eaten raw or cook after being peeled. It's full of vitamins and fiber.
4	**BLACK SPANISH RADISH**	You'll think you pulled up truffles when you harvest these unusual vegetables. This is another children's garden favorite because it looks so unusual. The orbs are larger than standard radishes—about the size of a handball—and matte black. The flavor is a bit spicier than other types of radishes.
5	**KARELA**	Karela is a type of bitter melon native to India and China. It looks like a spine-covered, eyeless prehistoric fish with a tiny tail. The texture and flavor of the flesh is closer to a cucumber than a melon, but inside the ugly exterior hides a stunning number of nutrients.
6	**SUNCHOKE**	Also called the "Jerusalem artichoke," the sunchoke is a tuber—closer in taste and texture to a potato than to an artichoke. The flavor is sweet and nutty and the vegetable can be eaten raw or cooked, and is even fermented and used to make an alcoholic drink. In any case, it looks like a knobby worm.
7	**RADICCHIO VARIEGATO DI CASTELFRANCO**	Radicchio is renowned for its lovely appearance. But this strange variety looks a little like a crime scene, with pale yellow leaves and what can only be described as red "blood spatter" across the leaves. However, the flavor is all traditional, bitter radicchio, and this variety is eaten in salads or roasted.
8	**DRAGON TONGUE BEAN**	This bush bean actually looks like what you might imagine a dragon's tongue looks like. The slightly misshapen bean is mottled all over with purple splotches. The flavor excels, and is considered superior to other bush beans.
9	**'GREEN ZEBRA' TOMATO**	One of my favorite tomatoes. You'll think it's not ripe, but it is. It is a beautiful chartreuse with deep lime-green stripes. The flesh is bright green and very rich tasting, sweet with a sharp bite to it (just too good to describe!). A favorite tomato of many high class chefs, specialty markets, and home gardeners.
10	**SPILANTHES**	Both the leaves and the gumdrop-shaped flower heads on this plant are edible. And both offer a mild shock to the tongue, an effect that no doubt contributes to the common name "Toothache Plant."

10 MOST POPULAR VEGETABLE SEEDS

Each year **W. Atlee Burpee & Company** fills their signature packets with millions of vegetable plants in the smallest possible form. As a storied seed company dating back to 1881, Burpee is well acquainted with seed bestsellers. In fact, Vegetable Product Manager Chelsey Fields can name the Top Ten performers without looking. As someone who regularly dives deep in the market data, Fields has some well-informed ideas of how top seed performers maintain their ranks on the list.

"In the past 15 to 18 years, we've slowly seen a transition from flowers to vegetables or edibles in home gardens. But as far as the edibles themselves, we see the time-honored favorites leading year after year," she said.

She thinks the allure is driven by consumers' desire to know where their food comes from and pride in growing their own. "They're looking at flavor and uniqueness of choice when it comes to homegrown versus store-bought."

Even within Burpee's top "classes" or species on the list, there is consistency except for new innovations. For instance, the recently introduced 'On Deck' corn—meant to be grown in a container—is popular for the need it fills. But the flavors of traditional bicolor sweet corn still make that tried-and-true standard a favorite. Ultimately, though, Fields understands seed popularity relates to simple food quality and the rewards of gardening.

"The number one is tomatoes. As far back as I've researched, it's always been tomatoes. You get some of the best flavor and some of the most interesting shapes," Fields said. "And though grocery stores are convenient, a grocery-store tomato can't really compare to one grown in your backyard. People see the difference in taste, juiciness, and even skin texture." Proof positive is Burpee's legendary 'Big Boy', released in 1949 and still in the company's Top Ten.

Other reasons drive the popularity of other Burpee offerings: beans, cucumbers, and squash. Fields thinks it comes down to practical considerations or seasonality and production. "Things like peas, cucumbers, and squash are really great for putting up. Can them, freeze them, and they're really nice for stretching your harvest into winter." But she also feels there is a less tangible appeal. "These are really good for the socialization aspect of gardening. There's always something to share. You can happily walk over to your neighbor with a full bag of produce to share, knowing you have even more coming." After all, if you want to be the winner in your garden, and your neighborhood, it only makes sense to plant a winner.

1   **TOMATO**

2   **BEAN**

3   **CUCUMBER**

4   **SQUASH**

5   **PEPPER**

6   **LETTUCE**

7   **CARROT**

8   **PEA**

9   **RADISH**

10   **SWEET CORN**

10 BEST VEGETABLES FOR CHALLENGING SOILS

Elizabeth Murphy literally wrote the book when it comes to soil. Her book, *Building Soil: A Down-to-Earth Approach: Natural Solutions for Better Gardens & Yards*, is a comprehensive guide to creating the perfect living medium for all your outdoor plants. She complements the book with her highly entertaining and informative blog, "Dirty Little Secrets" (www.dirtsecrets.com).

Murphy recommends a test as the first step to soil health. "A soil test is very helpful, especially starting out. The test determines if the soil lacks a necessary nutrient. For the serious home gardener, test every three years, or when you notice problems or a decline in production." She also suggests some simple guidelines for building good soil:

Provide necessary nutrients by testing soil and adding appropriate organic fertilizers.

Feed your soil (yes, the soil is a living thing) on a schedule, using bulky organic amendments as often as possible.

Keep your soil covered with mulch, living plants, organic amendments, or green manures.

Tests and amendments aside, Murphy says there's no substitute for becoming familiar with your soil. "Know your soil texture. That's defined as the amount of sand, silt, and clay, and determines the soil's properties. In soil with a high sand or clay content, modify what and how you grow to match the soil." See her specific plant suggestions on the right.

10 Best Vegetables for Drought Soils

1. **ASPARAGUS (ONCE ESTABLISHED)**
2. **BEAN**
3. **EGGPLANT**
4. **MUSTARD**
5. **OKRA**
6. **PEPPER**
7. **SQUASH (WINTER AND SUMMER)**
8. **TOMATO**
9. **AROMATIC HERBS (ROSEMARY, THYME, SAGE, OREGANO)**
10. **SWISS CHARD**

10 Best Vegetables for Clay Soils

Shallow-rooted vegetables can tolerate—and may even benefit from the stability of—heavy clays. Other root crops, like daikon radishes and potatoes, help to break up a heavy clay soil. Heavy clay soils are slow to warm, so planting early spring crops may not be possible.

1 **BROCCOLI**

2 **BRUSSELS SPROUTS**

3 **CABBAGE (RED AND GREEN)**

4 **CABBAGE (NAPA AND SAVOY)**

5 **CAULIFLOWER**

6 **KALE**

7 **BEAN**

8 **PEA**

9 **POTATO**

10 **DAIKON RADISH**

10 Best Vegetables for Sandy Soils

Crops with deep taproots crops love light, loose, and well-drained sands. These soils drain so rapidly, however, that even in water-abundant climates, vegetables suited for sandy soils must thrive in low-water and low-fertility conditions.

1 **CARROT**

2 **PARSNIP**

3 **BEET**

4 **RADISH**

5 **AROMATIC HERBS (ROSEMARY, THYME, SAGE, OREGANO)**

6 **ONION**

7 **GARLIC**

8 **POTATO**

9 **ASPARAGUS**

10 **TURNIP**

10 BEST VEGETABLES FOR WEIGHT LOSS

The trick to losing weight is to make sure you feel full and satisfied, while reducing the number of calories you take in. A secondary issue is the type of calories. Protein bars are all well and good, but they can be full of calories and additives that aren't exactly efficient for the body to use. Nature's weight-loss foods are the best way to go to ensure lasting results.

It's important to note that weight loss is a much more complicated issue than simply changing the foods you eat. We all want simple solutions, but even though weight loss begins with a basic calculation of calories in versus calories out, the picture quickly becomes more complicated. Other health issues can impact any weight loss program. That's why the very first step in losing weight is a visit to your doctor to ensure there are no underlying issues that you should consider before adjusting your diet.

Exercise also plays a part in a safe and effective weight loss program. One of the best forms of exercise is also one of the easiest and cheapest—walking.

The foods listed below can be added into your meals to aid in improving health and losing weight. (The two should always go hand-in-hand.) But it's a mistake to think of this as part of a "diet." The idea is to permanently change the way you eat, so that your weight loss and any improvements to your health are permanent as well. Lastly, keep in mind that your ideal weight is your ideal weight. It's determined by genetics, body type, and other factors and has nothing to do with magazine and TV ads.

1	**CUCUMBER**	High in water and low in calories, cucumbers are a refreshing snack that will keep you feeling light and energized. Make an incredibly tasty and soul-satisfying beverage by combining sliced cucumbers and lemons in a large pitcher of water. Keep it in the refrigerator and drink it throughout the day to maintain essential hydration.
2	**BROCCOLI**	Broccoli is considered one of many "low-density" vegetables—those that contain modest calories in relation to their fiber content. That means broccoli is a fat-free meal addition that features slow-release carbohydrates that will keep your energy high and your stomach feeling full. Cancer-preventing compounds are a big bonus with the vegetable that features less than 30 calories a serving.
3	**BEAN**	Bush and vine beans contain lots of fiber, a well-rounded flavor that satisfies hunger, and high amounts of protein that can provide a partial substitute for calorie-heavy red meat.
4	**CARROT**	Carrots are an ideal snack, simply cut into matchsticks or eaten whole. Buy heirloom or purple carrots to liven up your salads or as interesting between-meal snacks. Either way, the sweetness of the vegetable along with the fiber makes sure that you feel full and satiated.
5	**ZUCCHINI (SUMMER SQUASH)**	Roasted, steamed, grilled, sautéed, or eaten raw in salads, summer squashes have complex flavor and sturdy textures that will quickly fill you up and leave you very satisfied. They also provide a range of nutrients—to get the most out of them, cook with a variety of squash colors.
6	**RED PEPPER**	Sliced-up red peppers can be craving killers. Low in calories but high in natural sugars, a handful of red pepper slices can replace that late afternoon candy bar for a midday pickup. They have lots of water for necessary hydration and tons of vitamin C as well.
7	**ONION**	Key to losing weight is adding flavor to vegetarian and healthy meals. Onions, especially red onions, bring the flavor that will satisfy your hunger and your need for interest on the tongue as well.
8	**EGGPLANT**	This is a key low-density vegetable that can be used to replace other foods, such as chicken in pasta or veal in veal parmigiana. Grill it, steam it, or sauté it as you prefer.
9	**CAULIFLOWER**	Like broccoli, cauliflower offers tons of fiber in a nutrient-rich package that can be prepared in a number of ways. It's a filling flavor canvas that is delightful eaten raw, roasted, steamed, or even grilled.
10	**KALE**	You won't get bigger bang for your nutrition buck than with kale. Any leafy green is essential for the full feeling, but kale with its sturdy texture and strong flavor is king among leafy greens.

10 BEST VEGETABLES FOR OVERALL YIELDS

If you've got a big family to feed or you're the type of home gardener who likes to roll up her sleeves and put up like crazy when harvest comes in, you probably define quality of garden vegetables as the best yield. As much dollar-for-dollar benefit as herbs may return on your investment, chances are that you want pure quantity of usable food that can flat out fill the dinner-table platters and Mason jars.

This list is trickier to compile than it might seem. There are a lot of questions when looking at any plant's yield. Does it mature quickly, presenting opportunity for succession planting? Are there many fruits as opposed to one large fruit that is hard to use all at once? Are the fruits themselves relatively long lasting or can they be put up? Does the harvest come all at once, or spread out over the season?

Depending on the answers to these questions and many other issues, the order of vegetables that applies to your garden may be different than the one here. But the plants on the list probably won't change much in any case.

Boosting Your Yield

Whatever plants you grow in your garden, there are several steps you can take to ensure the biggest possible harvest.

Build good soil: Improving soil health will give your plants the best foundation for growing the strongest, most disease-free, and biggest vegetables possible. Soil should be rich in organic amendments such as compost, and should be a texture that allows for efficient drainage while retaining necessary moisture.

Go vertical: Many plants, from vining tomatoes to zucchini to cucumbers (and even melons!) will thrive on vertical supports if secured properly. The supports make the most of available space and allow for crucial air circulation that prevents disease.

Stretch your season: Succession planning coupled with cold frames or similar covers is a great way to stretch the growing season and possibly grow more than one crop in the same space over the season. Plan carefully to optimize the use of valuable garden real estate.

1 **TOMATO**

Choose indeterminate vining types and grow them up a trellis or support. Combine smaller types such as cherry or Roma with smaller hybrids to get a maximum number of tomatoes. Make and freeze sauces and put up extra for winter meals.

2 **POLE BEAN**

Although more work than bush types, pole beans produce a bumper crop that is easy to harvest and less prone to disease. Make sure the trellis or support will accommodate the weight and size of the mature vine, and look for the quickest-maturing varieties you can find.

3 **ZUCCHINI**

It's hard to top zucchini for sheer, almost out-of-control production. This is another plant that grows best on a vertical support. The trick is to have the kitchen ready to exploit the flood of zucchini when they ripen. Make bread, pickle them, shave them into zucchini spaghetti, and put up zucchini salsa for the colder months.

4 **CUCUMBER**

Choose vining cucumbers and grow them up a trellis, and look for smaller varieties that mature more quickly. If you'll be putting up some of your vegetable harvest, consider double-yield pickling varieties that can produce an astounding number of cucumbers.

5 **WINTER SQUASH**

The way to get the most squash possible off your vines is to choose small squash varieties, give them plenty of room to thrive, and start them inside just long enough before planting for the seedling to establish. Cure your harvest correctly and the squash will last through to spring.

6 **PEPPER**

Smaller sweet and hot peppers will produce more usable harvest than bell peppers. Some mature quickly, and almost all are suitable for canning. About a month before first frost, cut back top growth and flowers so that the plant puts its strength into the existing peppers and helps them mature quicker.

7 **LEAF LETTUCE**

Plant "cut and come again" lettuces for a continual harvest, and pick all leaves when small, on a regular basis, for a significant bounty of salad-bowl filler between your spring and fall harvests.

8 **RADISH**

Radishes are one of the fastest-maturing crops in the garden, and it's possible to harvest a month after you plant. Don't be shy about pulling your radishes slightly young—they'll be just as delicious. Plan for successive planting, and you'll get two to three crops between spring and fall plantings.

9 **CARROT**

Choose fast-maturing varieties, pick them young, and preserve the harvest you don't eat right away in a root cellar, by arranging individual carrots without touching, between layers of sand in a cool dry location like a basement.

10 **POTATO**

The secret to a huge crop of this filling tuber is layers and containers. Plant in a very deep raised bed or "potato bag," covering the seed potatoes with a layer of soil. Continue to add layers of soil covering the growing flower stem and by the end of season, you'll have layers of potatoes to harvest.

10 BEST EDIBLE FLOWERS

Rosalind Creasy, author of *The Edible Flower Garden* as well as a series of books on edible gardens, has done extensive research on flowers that cross the bridge from pretty to edible—as well as those that don't. People are often surprised at what she's discovered.

She's adamant about using a "caution first" approach. "You have to know your flowers. The American public is so used to seeing warning labels, that people often think because a flower is pretty it should be edible. The wrong flower can be toxic and even deadly. The very first rule should be: if you aren't absolutely certain it's edible, don't eat it. The second rule is: has it been sprayed with chemicals that are not allowed on edible plants? And finally, if the plant is new to you, start slowly and only consume a few petals to make sure you are not allergic to it."

---

1 BORAGE (*BORAGO OFFICINALIS*)

A native to Europe, this herb features blue star-shaped flowers with a subtle cucumber flavor. Use in syrups, vegetable and fruit salads, or candied to decorate desserts. Hold the stem in one hand and use the other to gently pinch the middle of the star and pull. The flower (*corolla*) should separate from the sepals intact. Warning! Pregnant and lactating women should avoid eating borage; as few as eight to ten flowers can cause milk to flow!

---

2 CALENDULA (*CALENDULA OFFICINALIS*)

Commonly known as pot marigolds, Roman peasants once used the crushed flowers as a substitute for expensive saffron. Use old-fashioned varieties like 'Pacific Beauty', not the new dwarf introductions. Calendula petals have a slightly tangy, bitter taste and are most often used for their color rather than flavor. Remove the petals from the 2-inch-wide heads and use whole or chopped, fresh or dried, in vinegars, soufflés, rice dishes, and omelets.

---

3 DAYLILY (*HEMEROCALLIS* SPP.)

You have to move quickly to take advantage of daylily flowers, which only bloom for a day (thus the name). The flavor ranges from sweet floral to slightly metallic, so taste before using. Daylily buds have long been used in Chinese stir-fries and Japanese tempura. Buds are chosen the day before they open and are added to hot and sour soup and are called "golden needles." They taste a bit like asparagus. Use sliced petals in salads and soups, or remove the stamens and pistils to stuff the whole flower with cheese and bread crumbs and sauté them.

4 LAVENDER (ENGLISH, AKA FRENCH) (LAVANDULA ANGUSTIFOLIA)

The strong lemon-perfume taste of the petals makes lavender excellent in simple syrups, sugars, vinegars, in a combination of herbs called *herbes de Provence*, and candied. Steep the leaves and flower heads for custard, lemonade, and ice cream.

5 NASTURTIUM (TROPAEOLUM MAJUS)

Pungent nasturtiums are popular edible flowers enjoyed since ancient Rome. The flowers, leaves, and seedpods are edible. The tangy flavor is mustard-like with an added sweetness. Harvest flowers just as they open. Mince and incorporate leaves and flowers into butter, oils, dressings, and vinegars. Sprinkle the petals over a green salad or use as a garnish.

6 PINKS (DIANTHUS SPP.)

Pinks are a form of carnation that have a pleasant, spicy, floral, clove-like taste. The 1- to 2-inch pink, red, or white blossoms can be steeped in wine, made into syrup or sorbets, custard, and used to garnish cakes, salads, soups, and the punch bowl. The bitter white base of the petals is removed.

7 ROSE (ROSA SPP.)

All roses are edible except heirlooms. *Rosa damascena*, the damask roses, are usually the most fragrant, and thus the most flavorful. Most roses offer a strong floral flavor, but some dark red varieties are unpleasantly metallic tasting. Remove the bitter white part at the base of petals. Individual petals of large varieties and the whole small-flowered roses can be candied and used as dessert garnish. The petals of fragrant roses have long been used to make jellies, rose water, vinegars, and infused to make flavored honey, butters, and simple and fruit syrups.

8 SQUASH BLOSSOM (CUCURBITA SPP.)

All squash and pumpkins produce large, edible yellow blossoms with a slightly sweet nectar taste. Wash and gently dry flowers (look out for bees, who sometimes get trapped inside). Blossoms for fritters or stuffing should have the stamens and pistils removed, but the stems left on. Stuff with cheese, breadcrumbs, and meat mixtures. Or thinly slice petals for soups, frittatas, pasta, and salads.

9 VIOLA, PANSY, AND JOHNNY-JUMP-UP (VIOLA CORNUTA, V. WITTROCKIANA, AND V. TRICOLOR)

The friendly faces of violas and pansies can be purple, pink, blue, yellow, and white. The petals taste a little like lettuce and can be used candied on desserts or fresh in salads. The petals can be made into simple syrup or infused into vinegar (and will turn the liquid lovely lavender).

10 VIOLET (VIOLA ODORATA)

The flowers have an intense, sweet, floral taste. They're great candied or plain on desserts, sprinkled on salads, as a garnish, and even to scent a sugar bowl, to flavor a custard, or to color and flavor a vinegar.

10 FASTEST-GROWING VEGETABLES

If you're worried about a short growing season in your region of the country, quickly changing temperatures or conditions, or you just want to have food as soon as possible after planting your garden, then you have a need for speed.

A speedy harvest can serve other purposes than just indulging the gardener's understandable impatience. Fast-growing vegetables are essential to keeping a young child's interest in a garden for kids. You want young ones to realize the bounty of their efforts as soon as possible. Quick-maturing plants like radishes and small carrots open up the possibility of succession planting that can greatly increase your overall harvest.

Some of the vegetables on this list have been included through a little gardening sleight of hand—they are picked early as baby vegetables. Still, you won't be sacrificing anything but size. Flavors and nutrition are just as good as in the fully mature versions.

There are, of course, other ways to get a jump on the season and get to harvest quicker. You can jumpstart your crops by starting them early in an ideal indoor location, or by growing mature seedlings in 3-inch pots. You'll spend more, but you cut time off the back end of your edible's life cycles.

1 **RADISH**

One of the reasons this crop is a favorite for kids' gardens is because radishes mature amazingly fast. Choose spring varieties for fully grown radishes in less than 30 days. Keep a bucket of sun-warmed water and you—or your children—can pick, wash, and eat the treats as a snack while gardening.

2 **SCALLION**

Scallions are essentially baby onions. Some varieties take less than 75 days to mature and the smaller onions are often much easier to integrate into salads and cooking than large bulb varieties. You can even harvest them slightly young, cutting even more time off the growing period.

3 **LETTUCE**

The fastest growing lettuces are loose-leaf varieties, which will be ready for harvest within eight weeks. Start harvesting even before then, by taking a few outer leaves to add to salads or use as garnish with other dishes. One of the great things about these lettuces is the amazing variety of flavors and textures available.

4 **SNAP AND SNOW PEA**

Choose smaller varieties that will mature 10 to 20 days earlier than more traditional sizes. The harvest will still be abundant, the flavor fresh and succulent.

5 **BUSH BEAN**

As with other plants, look for varieties that mature quickly; 'Provider' and 'Venture' are two that will grow beans ready for harvest in just over six weeks. Ensure the fastest germination and growth by soaking bush bean seeds in tepid water for 20 minutes prior to planting (don't oversoak or the beans will fall apart), and coating with inoculant right before putting the seeds in the soil.

6 **CUCUMBER (PICKLING VARIETIES)**

Both vine and bush types of cucumbers can be grown in containers, which gives you the chance to control the growing environment and speed up the time to harvest. Pick your variety carefully if speed is your top concern—some take as little as 48 days to mature.

7 **SPINACH**

One of the fastest and most nutritious leafy greens you can grow, spinach may be ready for harvest in as little as four to five weeks, depending on the variety you've chosen. The first leaves are ready to be cut as soon as they are big enough to eat. Keep harvesting the outer leaves as soon as you can use them and the bounty will keep on coming.

8 **KALE**

Warmer soil temperatures speed up kale growth, so use black plastic or other techniques to warm early spring soil and boost kale growth. Kale will also grow faster in very rich soil and in direct sun. To keep the speedy harvest on pace, immediately remove any mature leaves and don't allow them to yellow or wilt on the plant.

9 **TURNIP**

Watering turnips right after the seeds germinate will help the crop grow quicker, although this is already a quick-maturing vegetable. The quickest varieties will mature in a little more than 30 days, and you can begin harvest the leaves even while the root is growing, as soon as they are 10 inches or more.

10 **CARROT**

For the fastest carrot crop—around two months—grow ball or short varieties. However, carrots, like many other vegetables, are delightful when harvested very young. These are sweet and tender, and make wonderful side dishes to a main course of fish or meat.

10 BEST EDIBLES FOR SHADY GARDENS

Shaded locations are generally not ideal for growing a vegetable garden. Most edibles like to be bathed in sunlight while they grow. However, several different edibles can thrive in partial shade if they receive a bare minimum of strong direct sunlight for a given period during the day. Certain heat-averse plants can even benefit from the cooling effects of modest shade in the garden.

Generally speaking, you'll have more luck with edibles that you grow to harvest roots and leaves rather than fruits. This is especially true of leafy greens. In any case, check the varieties you choose carefully for those indicated to be shade tolerant.

Also keep in mind that many gardeners misjudge how much shade and sunlight a given area of a yard experiences. If you watch throughout the day, you may be surprised to find that a spot you thought was deeply shaded actually enjoys three to four hours of strong direct sunlight at one point or another. That's usually enough to grow many shade-tolerant edibles. Here are some suggestions to ensure success when growing edibles in shade.

Start plants indoors: Germinating seeds and getting plants established under optimal conditions will help them thrive in partial shade.

Prune nearby growth: Trim overgrown trees and shrubs near where you're planting the edibles. You may be surprised at how much additional sunlight the plants receive.

Grow near white or reflective surfaces: Sunlight does not necessarily have to be direct to be effective. Reflected sunlight can be every bit as beneficial to your edibles.

Containerize: Growing edibles in containers allows you move them as necessary to take advantage of whatever sun there is.

1 LETTUCE

Three hours of direct sun per day will usually be enough to grow a crop of leaf lettuces. Although the plants won't be as prolific as those grown in more abundant sunlight, they will also be less inclined to bolt—which may mean an additional week or more of harvesting the leaves.

2 SPINACH

The base minimum of sun for spinach to do well is four hours a day. Pick leaves early as baby spinach and a shady location will prevent bolting and lead to a significantly longer harvest period.

3 KALE

Kale is one of the best plants to grow in the shade and will be only slighter smaller than a full-sun plant. The leaves will be just as nutritious, though.

4 SWISS CHARD

Chard grown in shade generally produces smaller leaves, but the flavor and tenderness will be just as good as with the leaves of a large, sun-drenched plant.

5 BROCCOLI

Two to three hours of full sun is the minimum for this vegetable. But because it doesn't like heat, partial shade can actually benefit the plant.

6 BEET

Although you can grow beets in shade, they should ideally have more than four hours of direct sunlight per day. The less sun, the longer the root will take to mature.

7 RADISH

Although they do fine in full sun, radishes will also thrive in partial shade. They also do best in cooler temperatures, so shade that alleviates a hot sun in the middle of the day is ideal.

8 CARROT

Give carrots four hours of sun per day and they'll be fine—especially if you plant smaller varieties or harvest the root as a baby carrots, which will be delectable.

9 TURNIP

Turnips will tolerate a small amount of shade, but will not flourish in deep shade. A minimum of five hours of direct sun is best.

10 CABBAGE

Growing cabbage in partial shade is a trade-off. Although the plants will grow, the heads will be smaller and looser than they otherwise would have been. The ideal shade condition is one in which the plant starts out in full sun (such as under a tree that will leaf out as the weather warms), and then partial shade provides relief from hotter temperatures.

FAMILY NAMES OF VEGETABLES

Solanaceae—The nightshade family: tomato, pepper (sweet and hot), eggplant, tomatillo, and potato (but not sweet potato). Verticillium and fusarium wilt are common fungi that build in the soil when nightshades are planted in the same spot year after year.

Cucurbitaceae—The vining gourd family: cucurbits, cucumber, zucchini, summer and winter squash, pumpkin, melon, gourd.

Fabaceae—The legumes and nitrogen fixers: pea, bean, peanut, and cowpea.

Brassicacae—The cole crops, the mustard family, cool-season plants: broccoli, cauliflower, cabbage, kale, Brussels sprouts, radish, turnip, and collard greens.

Liliaceae—The onion family: onion, garlic, chive, shallot, or asparagus. When selecting a new site for asparagus beds, make sure that no other family members have been grown nearby for several years.

PHOTO CREDITS

RESOURCES

USDA Agricultural Research Service
www.ars.usda.gov

W. Atlee Burpee & Co.
www.burpee.com

Harris Seeds
www.harrisseeds.com

Johnny's Selected Seeds
www.johnnyseeds.com

Park Seed Company
www.parkseed.com

PlanGarden (yield and price calculator)
www.plangarden.com

Renee's Garden Seeds
www.reneesgarden.com

METRIC CONVERSION

Metric Equivalent

Inches (in.)	1/64	1/32	1/25	1/16	1/8	1/4	3/8	2/5	1/2	5/8	3/4	7/8	1	2	3	4	5	6	7	8	9	10	11	12	36	39.4
Feet (ft.)																								1	3	3 1/12
Yards (yd.)																									1	1 1/12
Millimeters (mm)	0.40	0.79	1	1.59	3.18	6.35	9.53	10	12.7	15.9	19.1	22.2	25.4	50.8	76.2	101.6	127	152	178	203	229	254	279	305	914	1,000
Centimeters (cm)							0.95	1	1.27	1.59	1.91	2.22	2.54	5.08	7.62	10.16	12.7	15.2	17.8	20.3	22.9	25.4	27.9	30.5	91.4	100
Meters (m)																								.30	.91	1.00

Converting Measurements

TO CONVERT:	TO:	MULTIPLY BY:	TO CONVERT:	TO:	MULTIPLY BY:
Inches	Millimeters	25.4	Millimeters	Inches	0.039
Inches	Centimeters	2.54	Centimeters	Inches	0.394
Feet	Meters	0.305	Meters	Feet	3.28
Yards	Meters	0.914	Meters	Yards	1.09
Miles	Kilometers	1.609	Kilometers	Miles	0.621
Square inches	Square centimeters	6.45	Square centimeters	Square inches	0.155
Square feet	Square meters	0.093	Square meters	Square feet	10.8
Square yards	Square meters	0.836	Square meters	Square yards	1.2
Cubic inches	Cubic centimeters	16.4	Cubic centimeters	Cubic inches	0.061
Cubic feet	Cubic meters	0.0283	Cubic meters	Cubic feet	35.3
Cubic yards	Cubic meters	0.765	Cubic meters	Cubic yards	1.31
Pints (U.S.)	Liters	0.473 (Imp. 0.568)	Liters	Pints (U.S.)	2.114 (Imp. 1.76)
Quarts (U.S.)	Liters	0.946 (Imp. 1.136)	Liters	Quarts (U.S.)	1.057 (Imp. 0.88)
Gallons (U.S.)	Liters	3.785 (Imp. 4.546)	Liters	Gallons (U.S.)	0.264 (Imp. 0.22)
Ounces	Grams	28.4	Grams	Ounces	0.035
Pounds	Kilograms	0.454	Kilograms	Pounds	2.2
Tons	Metric tons	0.907	Metric tons	Tons	1.1

Converting Temperatures

Convert degrees Fahrenheit (F) to degrees Celsius (C) by following this simple formula: Subtract 32 from the Fahrenheit temperature reading. Then mulitply that number by 5/9. For example, 77°F - 32 = 45. 45 × 5/9 = 25°C.

To convert degrees Celsius to degrees Fahrenheit, multiply the Celsius temperature reading by 9/5, then add 32. For example, 25°C × 9/5 = 45. 45 + 32 = 77°F.

Fahrenheit   Celsius

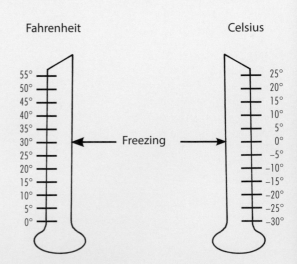

Fahrenheit	Celsius
55°	25°
50°	20°
45°	15°
40°	10°
35°	5°
30°	0°
25°	−5°
20°	−10°
15°	−15°
10°	−20°
5°	−25°
0°	−30°

Freezing

INDEX

artichoke, 31, 81
arugula, 30, 60
asparagus, 29, 31, 87, 103, 110, 111

basil, 39
  'Spicy Globe', 97
bean, 23, 29, 31, 85, 101, 109, 110, 111, 113
  Dragon Tongue, 107
beets, 31, 80, 99, 111, 121
  'Bull's blood', 97
bell pepper, 29, 89, 103, 105
borage, 116
Brassicacae family, 122
broccoli, 31, 76, 99, 111, 113, 121
  Romanesco, 107
Brussels sprouts, 29, 31, 90, 99, 103, 111
W. Atlee Burpee & Company, 108
bush bean, 23, 29, 31, 85, 101, 105, 119
  Dragon Tongue, 107

cabbage, 74–75, 99, 121
  green, 29, 31, 75, 111
  Napa, 31, 75, 111
  red, 31, 75, 111
  'Ruby Perfection', 97
  Savoy, 31, 74, 111
calendula, 116
cantaloupe, 30, 69
carrot, 70, 101, 109, 111, 113, 115, 119, 121
  heirloom, 31
  hybrid, 31
cauliflower, 31, 82, 111, 113
celery, 29, 31, 84
children's gardens, 100–101
chives, 37, 97
cilantro, 43
cold frames, 114
collard greens, 31, 72, 99
community gardens, 24
compost, 20
container gardens, 104–105
cooking techniques, for health, 98
corn, 31, 73, 101, 103, 109
Coronado, Shawna, 96

costs
  edible portions and, 12
  ledger for recording, 11
  per unit of produce, 12–13
  produce diversity and, 15–17
  regionality and, 17
  return on investment formula, 9
  USDA per pound averages, 13–14
  weather's effect of, 17
  See also expenses
Creasy, Rosiland, 116
cucumber, 30, 61, 101, 109, 113, 115
  Mexican Sour Gherkin, 107
  pickling, 119
Cucurbitaceae family, 122

Daikon radish, 31, 71, 111
daylily, 116
dill, 41
diversity, 15–17
drip irrigation systems, 23

eggplant, 30, 68, 103, 105, 110, 113
equipment, 19
expenses
  compost and, 19
  equipment, non-tool, 19
  labor, 23–24
  land and, 24
  soil amendments, 19
  tools, 17–18
  type of starter, 24–25
  water, 17, 21–23

Fabaceae family, 122
family names, 122
Farmers Market Coalition, 15
farmers' markets
  benefits and, 15
  costs and, 14–15
fascination gardens, 106–107
fennel (bulb), 30, 67
fermentation, 98
Fields, Chelsey, 108

Food Marketing Institute, 15
French tarragon, 38
garden investment ledgers, 11
garlic, 28, 30, 49, 111
grilling, vegetables for, 102–103

health benefits, 98–99
herbs, 28, 30–31, 32, 105, 110, 111
    See also individual types
hot pepper, 23

Jerusalem artichoke, 107
Johnny-jump-up, 117
juicing, 98

kale, 78, 99, 111, 113, 119, 121
    curly/purple/lacinato, 31
    dinosaur, 97
karela melon, 107
kohlrabi, 30, 66
    purple, 107

labor costs, 23–24
land costs, 24
lavender, 117
leek, 28, 30, 51
lettuce, 58–59, 101, 105, 109, 115, 119, 121
    butter, 30
    green/red leaf, 30
    mesclun, 30
    romaine, 30
Liliaceae family, 122
Lovejoy, Sharon, 100

mint, 36
    'Chocolate', 97
mulch, 23
Murphy, Elizabeth, 110
muskmelon, 30, 69
mustard, 110
mustard greens, 30, 54

nasturtium, 117

okra, 23, 29, 31, 86, 110
onion, 55–56, 103, 111, 113
    red, 30
    scallion, 119
    white, 30
    yellow, 30
oregano, 40
ornamental gardens, 96–97

pansy, 117
parsley, 44
    curly, 97
parsnips, 28, 30, 46, 111
pea, 77, 109, 111, 119
    snow, 31, 77, 119
    sugar snap, 31, 77, 99, 119
pepper, 99, 109, 110, 115
    bell, 29, 31, 89, 103, 105
    hot, 23
    ornamental, 97
    red bell, 113
pinks, 117
plant costs, 24–25
pole bean, 23, 29, 31, 85, 101, 115
potato, 29, 31, 91–92, 101, 103, 105, 111, 115
    red, 31
    russet, 31
    yellow, 31
produce diversity, 15–17
pumpkin, 30, 57, 101

radicchio, 30, 65, 103
    Variegato di Castelfranco, 107
radish, 31, 79, 101, 105, 109, 111, 115, 119, 121
    Black Spanish, 107
    Daikon, 31, 71, 111
rain barrels, 22–23
rainwater collection systems, 22–23
regional variations, 17
return on investment (ROI), 9, 30–31
rose, 117
rosemary, 23, 35, 97
row covers, 114

sage, 42
scallion, 119
seeds
    cost of, 24–25
    top vegetable, 108–109
shade
    tips for, 120
    vegetables for, 121
soil
    amendments for, 19
    tips or, 110
    vegetables for clay, 111
    vegetables for drought, 110
    vegetables for sandy, 111
    yield and, 114
Solanaceae family, 122
spilanthes, 107
spinach, 28, 30, 53, 99, 105, 119, 121
Square Foot Gardening
    lans costs and, 24
    produce cost numbers and, 13
    soil amendments and, 19
squash, 99, 109, 110
    blossoms of, 117
    summer, 9, 30, 64, 113
    winter, 28, 30, 52, 99, 115
strawberry, 30, 63
succession planning, 114
summer squash, 30, 64, 99, 110, 113
sunchoke, 107
supermarkets
    farmers' markets vs., 14–15
    USDA cost per pound for, 13–14
sweet potato, 31, 83
Swiss chard, 29, 31, 88, 105, 110, 121
    'Bright Lights', 97

tarragon, French, 39
thyme, 30, 34
tomato, 47–48, 101, 103, 105, 109, 110, 115
    cherry, 28, 30, 47
    Green Zebra, 107
    heirloom, 28, 30, 47
    hybrid, 28, 30, 47
    Roma, 30, 47–48
tools, 17–18
Toothache Plant, 107
turnip, 28, 30, 50, 111, 119, 121

unusual vegetables, 106–107
USDA Agricultural Marketing Service, 13

value
    bottom ten produce, 29
    children's gardens, 100–101
    container gardens, 104–105
    fascination gardens/unusual vegetables, 106–107
    fast-growing vegetables, 118–119
    formula for determining, 8–11
    grilling vegetables, 102–103
    health benefits, 98–99
    high yield vegetables, 114–115
    ornamental gardens, 96–97
    personal preferences and, 11
    produce by return on investment, 30–31
    return on investment formula, 9
    top seeds, 108–109
    top ten produce, 28
vertical growing, 114
viola, 117
violet, 117

water
    costs and, 18, 21–23
    low-water need produce, 23
    strategies for minimizing use, 22–23
watermelon, 30, 62, 101
weather, 17
weight loss, 112–113
winter squash, 28, 30, 52, 99, 110, 115

yield
    tips for boosting, 114
    vegetables for highest, 114–115

zucchini, 30, 64, 103, 113, 115

ABOUT THE AUTHOR

MEL BARTHOLOMEW'S PATH to arguably the most influential backyard gardener was an untraditional one. A civil engineer by profession and frustrated gardener by weekend, Bartholomew was convinced unmanageable single-row gardening was a waste of energy and output. After his research yielded responses such as, "But that's the way we've always done it," Bartholomew condensed the unmanageable single-row space to 4 x 4 feet, amended the soil, and bingo—he developed a gardening system that yields 100 percent of the harvest in 20 percent of the space.

Bartholomew's Square Foot Method quickly gained popularity and strength, ultimately converting more than one million gardeners worldwide. *Square Foot Gardening*, the highest-rated PBS gardening show to date, launched in 1981 and ran weekly for five years, followed later by a weekly *Square Foot Show* on the Discovery Network. In 1986, the creation of the Square Foot Gardening Foundation and the A Square Yard in the School Yard program brought the technique to an estimated three thousand schools nationwide.

As fan mail and testimonials from thousands of gardeners across the country arrived, Bartholomew realized that his Square Foot Method was relevant on a global scale. Converted into Square Meter Gardening, Bartholomew seized an opportunity to bring the dietary benefits of his revolutionary system to millions of malnourished Third World citizens. His global humanitarian effort, orchestrated through the Square Meter International Training Centers in Lehigh, Utah, and Homestead, Florida, trained international humanitarian organizations and leaders in the Square Meter Method. Since its launch, Bartholomew's global outreach initiative has spread from Africa to Asia to South America and is recognized as a resounding success by nonprofit human interest groups.

And there are no signs of slowing down. Bartholomew's global outreach continues throughout the world while closer to home, and attention has shifted to increasing the Square Foot presence in the California school system. Bartholomew is determined to continue and strengthen the well-established Square Foot programs and institutions across the nation and the globe.

Bartholomew operates his nonprofit Square Foot Gardening Foundation in Eden, Utah.